All In Good Ti

CW00506845

A Comedy

Bill Naughton

Helen Gmee

UÍVP F2

Samuel French - London
New York - Toronto - Hollywood

ALL IN GOOD TIME

First produced by The Mermaid Theatre Trust Ltd at The Mermaid Theatre, London, on the 6th March 1963, and subsequently, on the 18th April 1963, at The Phoenix Theatre, London, with the following cast of characters:

(in the order of their appearance)

LUCY FITTON, Arthur's mother	*Marjorie Rhodes*
EZRA FITTON, her husband	*Bernard Miles*
GEOFFREY FITTON, their younger son	*Edward Petherbridge*
JOE THOMPSON, Arthur's boss	*Peter Welch*
LIZ PIPER, Violet's mother	*Maureen Pryor*
MOLLY THOMPSON, Joe's wife	*Mary Quinn*
FRED STANFIELD, Violet's uncle	*John McKelvey*
ARTHUR FITTON, the bridegroom, Geoffrey's elder brother	
	John Pickles
EDDIE TAYLOR	*Bunny May*
VIOLET FITTON, the bride	*Lois Daine*
LESLIE PIPER, Violet's father	*Donald Eccles*

Directed by JOSEPHINE WILSON

Designed by DAVID MYERSCOUGH JONES

SYNOPSIS OF SCENES

ACT I

SCENE 1 The Fittons' home in Bolton. The night of the wedding. Spring.
SCENE 2 The same. Thursday night. Six weeks later.
SCENE 3 The same. The following morning

ACT II

SCENE 1 The same. The evening of the same day ⎫ For alternative
SCENE 2 Fred's garden. The following morning ⎬ setting see section
SCENE 3 A piece of waste ground. A few hours later ⎭ at end of play
SCENE 4 The Fittons' home. That evening

Time—the present

The song in Act I is "Roses" by F. E. Weatherly and Stephen Adams, published by Boosey and Hawkes Music Publishers Ltd, 295 Regent Street, London, W.1

ACT I

SCENE I

SCENE—*The Fittons' home in Bolton. The night of the wedding. Spring.*

The Fittons' home is a cottage house in an industrial street. The setting shows the living-room with a bedroom above. It is furnished in a homely mixture of old and new, with a prosperous and cosy appearance, and has signs of having been newly decorated for the wedding and has a warm, festive air, with simple touches of a house-proud wife here and there. In the living-room, a door L leads to the street. An arch up R leads to the kitchen and stairs. The fireplace is down R with a window above it. In the bedroom, the door, with a curtained glass panel, is up L and leads first into another bedroom and thence to the stairs. There is a small window L. In the living-room, below the fireplace, there is a fireside stool and a pouffe, and above the fireplace is a small table with a TV set. A comfortable old leather armchair stands above the fireplace. A sideboard, L of the door up R is loaded with wedding presents, a bottle of port, some glasses, a plate of cakes, boxes, and ornaments, etc. An upright piano is up L with a chair in front of it. Another chair stands R of the piano. On top of the piano there are glasses, beer, sandwiches, a jug of spring flowers and a concertina. Along the wall L, above the street door, there is a row of pegs loaded with coats and hats. Below the street door there is a small table with a record player on top, and on the lower shelf, books and a transistor radio. In the corner down L, there is a piano stool and a keg of beer resting on two crates, a large jug of ale and some glasses. A square dining-table covered with a red plush cloth, is C. Three chairs, one R, one L, and one above the table, are well tucked in. At night, the room is lit by a pendant light C, and a table-lamp on the piano. In the bedroom, the bed is R, along the back wall, the head of the bed R. Violet's nightdress and Arthur's pyjamas are on the pillow and Violet's wedding veil is over the foot of the bed. The left end of the bed is so constructed that it will collapse when Arthur sits on it, after Joe has loosened the bolts. A box ottoman is at the foot of the bed, set to conceal the "collapsing" legs. Below the bed, R, is a bookcase with books and on the top a bedside lamp and a bunch of roses. Below the bed is a small chair and a rug. Up LC, against the back wall, there is an enamel bowl on a washstand with a water carafe in it. A towel hangs on the rail of the washstand. There is a shelf fixed to the wall over the washstand with a tumbler, shaving-brush, shaving-stick, etc. The washstand is concealed by a folding screen covered with portraits of composers, soiloists and reprints of famous art treasures, etc. Arthur's dressing-gown hangs on a hook behind the door. A small dressing-table and mirror stands in front of the window, with a lace cover and a few toilet articles. A rug covers the floor area LC. Below the ottoman stands a small table with a tape-recorder on it.

Before the CURTAIN *rises, soft, muted Irish jig music is heard.*

The CURTAIN *rises on a lively scene at the end of a wedding party, and it is after midnight. The lights are on in the living-room and the bedroom is in darkness. The record player is blaring out a brisk Irish jig.* EZRA FITTON *is dancing with* MOLLY THOMPSON *above the table* C. EZRA, *aged fifty, the bridegroom's father, is a gasworks labourer. He appears to be a stubborn and loud-mouthed man on first sight. Later, however, he reveals unsuspected depths of character and feeling, and it becomes evident that he is a more complex person that he would have anyone know.* MOLLY, *aged thirty-six, is lively and gay.* GEOFFREY FITTON *and* EDDIE TAYLOR *are "twisting" up* L. GEOFFREY, *aged twenty-four, is Arthur's younger brother, a mechanic, big and cheery.* EDDIE, *aged eighteen, is a simple young lad who works with Arthur.* FRED STANFIELD *is standing* L *of the table, with a glass of beer, laughing and keeping time.* FRED, *Violet's uncle, is aged fifty-two. He is a physiotherapist, and is a rather earnest man.* JOE THOMPSON *and* LIZ PIPER *are dancing down* L. JOE *is a cinema manager, aged forty. He is Arthur's boss. He is fond of a joke.* LIZ, *aged forty-five, is Leslie's wife. She is fussy, and a bit fancy, but no fool.* LUCY FITTON *is standing at the arch up* R. LUCY, *aged fifty, is a shrewd, unfussy working-class mother, with a dry humour and a good heart beneath her tough front.* VIOLET FITTON *and* LESLIE PIPER *are standing up* R. VIOLET *is aged twenty, simple, attractive and genuine. She wears a short length bridal dress.* LESLIE, *aged forty-eight, is an insurance collector. He is rather measured, but under pressure reveals what conflict has been going on underneath.* ARTHUR FITTON, *the bridegroom is seated on the stool down* R, *reading a book and taking no notice of the din. He is aged twenty-five and is a cinema projectionist with a natural taste for good music and reading, and is often at a loss amongst his own folk.* JOE *and* LIZ *dance* L *of the table, then above it, and stop.* VIOLET *and* LESLIE *exit to the kitchen.* EZRA *and* MOLLY *dance down* R. EZRA *swings* MOLLY *round from side to side and the others, all except* ARTHUR, *egg him on, forming a semicircle of spectators,* L *of the table. There is shouting and laughter, all rather "merry". After a moment,* LUCY *calls to Geoffrey.*

LUCY. Hey, turn that thing down.

(GEOFFREY *goes to the record player and unwillingly turns down the volume.* LUCY *just avoids being bowled over by the dancing* EZRA, *gives a snort and exits to the kitchen.* EZRA *becomes aware that the music has gone down and stops dancing*)

EZRA. Hey, who's turned that music down?
GEOFFREY. My mum said . . .
EZRA. Never mind what your mum said—turn it up again. I'm the boss in this house.
JOE. Good old Ezra—that's the spirit.

(GEOFFREY *turns up the volume*)

LIZ. You've got to think of the neighbours, Mr Fitton.
EZRA. To hell with the neighbours—we owe 'em nowt.

(*The music is lively and gay.* EZRA *swirls off again with* MOLLY. *The shouts and yells restart.* EZRA *has not gone more than a few steps when the*

pouffe gets in the way and he falls headlong towards the armchair, taking
Molly *with him.* Arthur *rises.* Fred *crosses and helps* Ezra *to rise.*
Joe *picks up* Molly *and they move to the sideboard. The others help,*
with shouts of sympathy. Eddie *turns off the record player and there is a*
sudden silence. After his brief glory, Ezra *looks like a man who has come*
a cropper)

Liz. Ee, are you all right, Mr Fitton?
Molly. He let with such a bang.
Fred. Yes—a heavy fall. How do you feel?

(*They are all concerned but* Ezra *shakes them off*)

Geoffrey. Are you all right, Dad?
Ezra (*dazedly rubbing his head*) Yes, I'm all right.
Liz. Are you sure you're all right?
Joe. He went ass over tip.
Ezra (*shouting*) I tell you I'm all right. Leave me alone.

(Fred *moves up* R)

Geoffrey (*whispering*) Leave him alone if he says so.
Ezra (*staring at Arthur*) Hy, did you trip me up deliberate?
Arthur. Me? I didn't trip you at all.
Ezra. I fell over somebody's foot.
Arthur. Then it must have been your own. I didn't even see you.
Ezra. I'm not a chap to fall over my own foot.
Molly. You fell over the pouffe.
Ezra. I coulda swore I saw a foot stuck out as I was coming round.
Arthur (*sitting on the stool*) I tell you I wasn't even looking.
Eddie. Arthur was reading, Mr Fitton. (*He sits on the chair up* L)
Ezra. *Readin'* on his weddin' night—a son of mine! I never thought I'd live to see the day. (*He crosses to* L, *takes a glass of beer from the table* L *and sits on the piano stool*)
Molly (*friendly*) Happen he's readin' it up, eh, y'know . . .

(*There is general laughter*)

Liz. He's left it bit late.
Joe. It's one of them jobs, the more y'know about it the worse you are at it. (*He cackles. He has a way of breaking off suddenly*)
Molly. It's certainly true in your case.
Fred. She's got you there, mate—she should know.

(*The others laugh at* Joe. Arthur, *put off by this talk, turns back to his book with some annoyance*)

Ezra (*rising and moving above the table*) Hy, are you readin' that book again?
Arthur. What about it if I am?
Ezra (*crossing to* RC *and turning to the others*) Look at him—he's like a flamin' ghost at his own weddin'.

ARTHUR. What would you like me to do—stand on my bloody head?

LIZ. Arthur! Language! Talking like that to your father!

EZRA. Thank you, Mrs Piper. (*He moves closer to Arthur*) No, but I expect you to make a bit of jollification on your weddin' night. (*In a loud whisper*) These folks is your guests—Joe Thomson your boss here.

ARTHUR (*rising; to the others*) I'm sorry, everybody. (*He smiles*) I just thought you could manage better without me.

FRED. It's all right, lad. I dare say you're tired.

EDDIE. Aye, he's been married, hasn't he?

GEOFFREY. It's a tiring job.

MOLLY. It's been a long day for you, love.

ARTHUR. It's all right. It's just that I can't stand all that din.

(JOE *crosses to the barrel down* L *and helps himself to beer*)

EZRA (*shouting*) Din! We were dancing, and he has the cheek to call it din. An' put that bloody book down when folk are talkin' to you.

(FRED *moves and sits on the stool down* R)

ARTHUR. Can't you speak without shouting?

EZRA. I'll speak as I think fit in my own house.

GEOFFREY. Don't excite yourself, Dad. I'll handle him. (*He crosses to* R *of Arthur; big and confident*) Giss that book.

ARTHUR (*with elder brother authority*) You keep off!

GEOFFREY. The trouble he's caused in this house with his reading.

EDDIE (*rising*) Be careful, Geoff . . .

EZRA. Look at him—a book in his hand on his weddin' night. Who ever heard of such a thing.

ARTHUR. Oh, dry up!

LIZ. Arthur, that's no way to speak to your father.

EZRA. Thank you, Mrs Piper. (*He prods Arthur*) Until you get a place of your own, my boy, don't forget I'm the boss in this house.

ARTHUR (*meaning it*) I'll go now if it'll suit you. I can pack my things in five minutes—and be out of here. (*He calls*) Violet! Come on!

GEOFFREY. Don't be daft, Arthur. (*To Ezra*) You'll catch it from my mum if he does go.

EZRA. Harken him! (*He moves* C) See how he turned on me. What have I said? (*He is thoroughly discomfited at the way things are turning out. He knows he will get into trouble with his wife for one thing, and also, he likes Arthur*)

EDDIE (*crossing to* L *of Arthur*) Don't worry, Mr Fitton. Leave him to me.

(EDDIE *and* GEOFFREY *restrain Arthur*)

EZRA. There y'are, you say a word to them and they threaten to walk out. I'd never have spoke to my dad like that. But that's a son's gratitude these days. (*He is such a mixture of the braggart and the genuine that you are never quite sure of him*)

Arthur. You don't want me to be grateful to you for being born, do you?

Ezra (*quietly*) You might be grateful to me for a lot of things one day—if truth were known.

(Arthur *senses a deep meaning behind Ezra's words and father and son stare at each other in silence for a moment. The others watch silently.*

Lucy *enters from the kitchen, carrying a tray of tea which she puts on the table* c)

Lucy. If what truth were known? (*She moves to* R *of Ezra*)

(*An odd, sad look comes over* Ezra. *He remains silent, crosses to the piano stool* L *and sits*)

Molly (*crossing to* Ezra) He's saying nothing. Are you, Mr Fitton? (*She puts a comforting hand on Ezra's shoulder*)

Lucy. Happen it's as well. (*She sits* R *of the table* c *and sets out the tea things*)

(Leslie *and* Violet *enter from the kitchen, breaking the tension.* Leslie *is carrying the wedding cake. The cake already has a piece cut out of it.* Violet *carries a plate and knife.* Liz *reacts irritably at the sight of father and daughter together*)

Liz (*moving to* L *of Leslie*) I wondered where you two had got to.

Leslie. I was just having a little last chat to our Violet. (*He looks for somewhere to put the cake, but is in no hurry to put it down*)

(Geoffrey *and* Eddie *cross above the others and stand up* L. Fred *rises and moves to the fireplace.*

Molly *crosses and exits to the kitchen*)

Liz. You do nothing but chat, you two. What're you walkin' about with that in your hands for? Put it down.

(Arthur *sits on the stool down* R. Violet *puts the plate and knife on the sideboard.* Eddie *sits on the chair up* L)

Leslie. I will if you'll show me where.

Liz. The way you're takin' things on yourselves, anybody would think it was your wedding.

(Geoffrey *joins Fred at the fireplace.* Joe *moves up* L)

Leslie. It's my daughter's.

Liz. She's my daughter, too. Put it down.

Violet (*turning to* Liz) Mum, love, don't keep pickin' at Dad.

Liz. Nobody's pickin' at him, love. But look at him—the way he's actin' with that weddin' cake anybody would think he was goin' to take it home with him an' put it under his bloomin' pillow.

Leslie. Where can I put it?

Liz. I'd love to tell you!

Violet. Mum, Dad was only helping me.

LESLIE. It's all right, Violet. Don't argue with your mother.

VIOLET. Here, Dad, put it over here on the dresser.

(LESLIE *puts the cake on the sideboard.*

MOLLY *enters from the kitchen, carrying a jug of hot water. She puts the jug on the table then assists* LUCY *to serve the tea*)

LESLIE. Will it be all right here, Mrs Fitton?

LUCY. Yes, it won't get knocked off there. Tea, Molly? (*To Ezra*) What's bitten you?

MOLLY. It was to do with your Arthur.

EZRA. Aye, your son there was readin' a flamin' book.

LUCY. He's your son as well as mine. Why shouldn't he read? Tea for you, Mrs Piper? He's doing nobody any 'arm.

LIZ. Yes, please. (*She sits* L *of the table* C)

EZRA. Readin' a book at his own bloomin' weddin'—who ever heard of it.

LUCY. Why shouldn't he? Tea, Mr Piper?

LESLIE. Yes, please, Mrs Fitton.

EZRA. I was never brought up to read at weddin's.

LUCY. You! You couldn't see on your weddin' night. Sugar, Mr Piper?

LESLIE. Two, please. He only meant it for the lad's good.

EZRA. 'Course I did, I only wanted to see the lad happy.

LUCY. He's always on at our Arthur.

ARTHUR. Mother, do be quiet! Please!

EZRA. I hardly ever speak to him. It's you, you've spoilt him—marded him. Since he were that high.

ARTHUR. Here we go again.

LUCY. You don't notice yourself doin' it. Tea, Mr Thompson? But others do.

EZRA. You've made a mardarse out of him. That's what you've done.

MOLLY. Mr Fitton, that's not true. He's a right good lad is your Arthur.

VIOLET. Thank you, Molly. I agree. (*She cuts the cake*)

ARTHUR. Please leave me out of it.

LUCY. Even on the lad's weddin' night, you've got to pick on him.

(VIOLET *puts a plate of cut cake on the table* C)

Help yourselves to cake.

EZRA. I didn't pick on the lad. He picked on me. He tripped me up.

EDDIE. Excuse me, but he did not. You fell over the pouffe, Mr Fitton. I saw you.

FRED. And so did I.

EZRA. I'm not a chap to fall. I'm too nimble on my feet.

LUCY. He's about as nimble as a baby elephant.

GEOFFREY. Let's change the bloomin' subject.

ARTHUR. I should think so.

JOE. Heah! Heah! Two sugars for me, Mrs Fitton. Eddie, get me a cup of tea, will you?

(EDDIE *rises, gets a cup of tea and hands it to Joe, then collects a cup for himself and resumes his seat on the chair up* L)

EZRA (*reasonably*) All this sittin' readin' and thinkin' can't be any good for anybody. It's not natural.

ARTHUR (*rising*) Oh, blimey—off we go again. (*He collects a cup of tea and stands up* C)

(VIOLET *collects her tea and joins Arthur up* C)

EZRA (*striving to be reasonable*) It's not—I tell you it's not.

LUCY. I wish you'd try it for a change. Have you all got tea?

EZRA. My dad used to say, if a thing's natural you'll see animals doin' it. I've yet to see a horse readin' a flamin' book.

(*The others laugh*)

LUCY. You might—if you live long enough.

EZRA. Or a dog with a newspaper. Then suppose one day he should overstrain his brain—eh?

LUCY. That's something you'll never do. (*She indicates the cake*) Help yourselves, everybody. (*She sips her tea*)

FRED. Speaking as a physiotherapist—I don't think you can overstrain the brain that easy.

EZRA. Oh, don't you? Well, speaking as a gasworks labourer I beg to differ. What about that chap in the paper whose brain busted?

LUCY. I know where you'll bust if ever you do—an' it won't be your brain.

LESLIE. If it's in Arthur's nature to read you've got to give way to it—or it'll come out some other road.

ARTHUR. I tell you, leave me out of it, please.

LIZ. I think Mr Fitton only meant it for Arthur's good.

EZRA (*rising and crossing down* R) 'Course I did. I want to see the lad havin' a good time. It gripes me to see anybody struggling with the printed word. (*He sits on the stool down* R)

LUCY. More tea, anyone. (*To Arthur*) What about you, love?

ARTHUR. Yes, Mum. (*He moves to the table* C)

(LUCY *refills Arthur's cup*)

EZRA (*to Arthur*) Are you havin' a pint with me, lad, a pint of ale? Eh, come on. (*He rises*)

ARTHUR. All right, Dad—I will.

EZRA. Good lad—I'll draw a pint for you myself.

ARTHUR. Oh, sorry, Dad—I'd rather have a cup of tea, if you don't mind. Ale gives me a headache at this time of night.

EZRA (*rebuffed*) Harken him—I'd rather have a cup of tea. I'm suppin' no tea whilst there's ale in the barrel. Who's for ale? What about you, Joe? (*To Geoffrey*) An' you? (*To Fred*) An' you?

Joe (*collecting his glass*) Aye, ale for me. (*He crosses to the barrel, refills his glass then moves up* L)

Geoffrey. Me, too. What about you, Fred?

Fred. I'll stick to tea.

Ezra. Come on, Geoff, hand 'um out. My old father 'ud turn in his grave at the idea of a Fitton preferring tea to ale.

Eddie. I'll have ale. (*He rises*)

(Geoffrey and Eddie *put their cups on the table* c, *collect their glasses, move down* L *and refill their glasses with ale. They then take a piece of cake each and move up* L. Molly *moves* L)

Leslie. I think I'll have a drop of port. (*He helps himself from the bottle on the sideboard*)

Fred (*moving to* R *of Arthur*) I hear you're going in for joining the police force, Arthur?

Violet (*moving and sitting above the table* c, L *of Arthur*) Yes, won't it be nice.

Joe. Aye, he'd be as well—our little cinema might close down any day. Then he'll be looking for a job.

(Molly *takes the plate of cake to Ezra and offers it to him.* Ezra *takes a piece of cake*)

Arthur. Aye—I fancy an open-air life.

Ezra. Ale gives him a headache—ale never gave anybody a headache.

Lucy. Once he gets a thing on his mind he never lets go.

Geoffrey. They've sent him back twice—he's half an inch short.

Leslie. No telling what marriage might do.

Liz. Marriage—why you seem to have shrunk since I wed you.

Violet. Not surprising—eh, Dad?

Liz. Don't be cheeky. They're a pair these two are.

Fred (*crossing up* L) There's a good pension after twenty-five years. You could retire at fifty.

Arthur. Aye, I suppose you could. I never thought of that—you could have another job on top of your pension.

Ezra. Harken him—he's talkin' of bloody retirin' before he's even started on the job.

Arthur. I never talked of it—I only agreed with Fred here.

Lucy. 'Course you did, love.

Fred. To be sure he did.

Ezra. That's the youth of today all over—they ask about pension afore they get the bloody job.

Violet. He didn't, Mr Fitton. He only said . . .

Ezra (*crossing up* L) There's never been a one of my family joined the police force—I can say that.

Lucy. If they were anything like you they couldn't join the library.

Ezra. I could get him a job alongside me at the gasworks. He won't come, will he?

(ARTHUR *moves to the stool down* R *and sits*)

LESLIE. Young men don't go into labouring jobs these days.
FRED. A spade is a thing of the past.
EZRA. It'll be the end of this country once a chap can't use a spade. Who ever heard of a navvy with a headache? Projectionist! Policeman!
FRED. If he fancies the police I can't think why he shouldn't join.
EDDIE. Aye, it's no joke with all the hoodlums about these days.
LUCY. No use talking—he won't listen.

(MOLLY *moves and stands* R *of Violet*)

ARTHUR. Keep me out of it, Eddie.
GEOFFREY. They've not taken him on yet.
EZRA (*to Fred*) You don't see my side of it. Suppose it gets out amongst my mates at the gasworks as it certainly will, a copper in the family. Eh? I'd never live it down.
GEOFFREY. He's not on the force yet, Dad.
EZRA. That's even worse—a bloody *failed* copper in the family. Come on, chaps, gather round for more ale.
JOE. Did I tell you the tale about the twin Chinamen on their honeymoon?
EZRA. I'll bet there were a right mix-up there. Ha! Ha! Who ever heard of ale giving you a headache, eh?

(ARTHUR *sits alone as the* MEN *gather up* L, *whispering and laughing. The* WOMEN *are around the table*)

VIOLET. Ee, Mum, it'll seem funny, saying good night to you and Dad and seeing you off.
LIZ (*dabbing her eyes*) My little girl.

(*The* MEN *whisper and laugh together*)

VIOLET. What's up with you, Mum?
LUCY. It's a big moment for a mother, love, her daughter's first night.
LIZ. It brings it all back. Look at her. I can't believe she's married.
MOLLY. She does look young for her age, bless her.
LIZ. I feel there's so much I could have told her, but somehow I never got round to it.
LUCY. It's all there—but you can't get yourself to say it.
VIOLET. It's all in detail in that book I got.
MOLLY. Book! Why, one proper encounter with a chap will tell you more than a dozen books.
LUCY. Aye, there's all the difference in the world between theory and practice in that field, love.
LIZ. It's the hints that count, love—hints that only a mother can give.
MOLLY (*whispering to Violet*) I'll give you two now—never show pleasure—men are such prudes, see—every one of 'em . . .

LIZ. Not that there ever is much.

MOLLY. Spoken from the heart.

LUCY. Hush up—you're making little Violet embarrassed with your talk.

MOLLY. But never refuse a man point-blank—they take it out of your housekeeping money.

LIZ. That's never been one of my problems.

MOLLY. I see what you mean.

LUCY. Shame on you—you're shocking the little girl.

MOLLY (*looking at Violet*) Ee, doesn't she look bonny when she blushes?

LIZ. She's innocent—although I say it myself as shouldn't. Her dad wouldn't let the *News of the World* into the house.

VIOLET. Mum! You know I can't stand all this sort of talk.

MOLLY. Arthur—you're one of the lucky ones—you've got an innocent wife.

(ARTHUR *decides to join the Men and rises, but a big belly laugh from the group at that moment puts him off.* EDDIE *sees him react and looks regretful.* ARTHUR *crosses to the front door* L, *turns there and catches* VIOLET'S *eye and beckons her to follow him.*

ARTHUR *exits by the front door.* JOE *starts to sing "I Wish I Were Single Again"*)

LIZ. See—men don't like to hear it.

MOLLY. It's just that Arthur's way.

LUCY. He's a good lad and he'll make a good husband. I shall miss him when he goes.

(VIOLET *rises and exits quietly by the front door*)

LIZ. She's a good girl—but I'll be glad to see her go. Her and her dad, see, they're on the same wavelength, they have their little jokes together.

(*The* MEN *join in the singing and it reaches a loud pitch*)

MOLLY. I heard 'em back there. It can make you feel shut out when they play that game.

MEN (*singing*)
        "My wife got the fever, Oh then, Oh then,
        My wife got the fever, Oh then.
        Oh my wife got the fever
        And I had to leave her
        And I wished I were single again.

        Oh I wish I were single again
        I wish I were single again.
        I wish I were single
        My pockets would jingle
        My pockets would jingle again.

        My wife she did die, Oh then, Oh then . . ."
        (*Etc.*)

LUCY. Hy, stop it.

LIZ. Turn it up.

(*The singing stops*)

EZRA. What's up?

MOLLY. Can't you find a better song for a wedding night?

LIZ. You've driven the poor bridal pair out in the street.

(JOE *whispers to Geoffrey and indicates the door up* R. GEOFFREY *shakes his head*)

LUCY. Ezra, sing us one of the old songs—like you used when we were first married.

LIZ. Yes, Mr Fitton, let's hear you sing for a change.

MOLLY. Yes, love, and I'll accompany you.

EZRA. Can you play *Roses?*

MOLLY. I can play owt if you can sing it. (*She crosses to the piano, sits at it and plays the air*)

JOE. I told you she was a good girl at a party.

EZRA. That was my old mate's favourite song. I'll sing it in memory of our friendship. Don't pitch it too high.

(MOLLY *plays the introduction clear and well.* EZRA *stands ready to sing.* JOE *takes Geoffrey by the sleeve, whispers to him and leads him up* R. GEOFFREY *nods*)

GEOFFREY. I'll turn the light off, Dad—it'll sound sweeter.

FRED. Aye, it's nice is a song in the firelight glow.

EZRA. Help me out, everybody—when I get stuck.

(GEOFFREY *switches off the lights and the room is lit by the glow of the fire*)

(*He sings in an unexpectedly clear tenor voice*)

> "I'll send thee red, red roses
> To tell thee of the morn,
> When first amongst the roses
> Our happy love was born,
> Our happy love was born.
> I'll send thee white, white roses,

(JOE *and* GEOFFREY *sneak out of the room and go up the stairs into the bedroom*)

> To tell thee of the night
> The night in all its beauty
> With all its dreams and light
> The night with all its beauty
> With all its dreams and light
> With all its dreams and light.

(*There is clapping and applause from the others.*

EDDIE *follows Joe and Geoffrey up the stairs.* JOE *and* GEOFFREY *appear in the bedroom.* JOE *switches on the lights in the bedroom. The following scene, over the singing, is a silhouetted blend of ballet and mime, punctuated by shrieks and guffaws from* JOE. *He picks up the bridal veil and puts it on his head. He takes a flimsy nightdress off the bed and mimics a shy bride with* GEOFFREY. *The cover is flung off the bed and the mattress is pulled back, then a spanner is waved and they begin to unfasten the bolts on the bed, making signals of silence at their lips.* EDDIE *enters the room and creeps up on the conspirators. They jump back in alarm.* EDDIE *tries in vain to prevent them from fixing the bed. During all this the song swells up from below with strong old-fashioned sentiment, the others joining in*)

LESLIE. Another verse—and we'll all join in.

ALL.
> And when thou seest the roses
> This will the roses say,
> There is no day without thee,
> No night when thou'rt away,
> No night when thou'rt away.
> No day I do not love thee
> No night I do not pray
> That God will bless and guard thee,
> For ever night and day,
> That God will bless and guard thee
> For ever night and day,
> For ever night and day.

(*During this last chorus,* JOE, GEOFFREY *and* EDDIE *come from the bedroom and into the living-room.* EDDIE *is last out of the bedroom and switches off the lights. They join in loudly in the song and the cheering and clapping which follows at the end of it*)

GEOFFREY. I'll put the light on, Dad. (*He switches on the living-room lights*)

EDDIE. You've a right good voice, Mr Fitton.

EZRA. I had once, lad, in my young days—I'd a fair singing voice, and me and my old mate, Billy Stringfellow, we'd go into any pub in town and challenge the best pair in the place to a singing match.

GEOFFREY. What—sing 'um, Dad, not fight 'em?

FRED. Folk were civilized in them days.

EZRA (*crossing down* R) Billy always wanted to sing 'um first—for pints—but if they were the fighting sort he'd fight 'em just as happily. What a mate! He'd fight whilst he'd breath in his body—or he'd sing.

LUCY (*sharply*) Do we have to bring Billy up tonight?

EZRA. Why shouldn't I bring him up?

LUCY. Because nobody knows him and nobody wants to hear about him.

(MOLLY *collects the cup and saucers and puts them on the tray*)

GEOFFREY. Who were Billy, Dad?

LUCY. Nobody.

EZRA. Don't say that, Lucy.

Geoffrey. I was talking to my dad.
Lucy. Yes, and I'm answering for him.
Ezra. Not for the first time, either. I bloody knew him, didn't I?

(Ezra *and* Lucy *look at each other with a certain deep significance.*
      Arthur *and* Violet *enter* l. Violet *moves down* l. Arthur
closes the door)

(*He looks across and stares at Arthur. To Lucy*) And so did you.
Lucy (*rising*) Don't drive me too far—I'm warning you.

(Lucy *picks up the tray and exits to the kitchen*)

Geoffrey. He sounds a rum 'un, does Billy.

(Liz *rises and exits to the kitchen.*
      Molly *follows her off*)

Ezra. A decenter lad never wore shoe leather. And he were the
all-time champion at the elbow game.
Eddie. What's the elbow game, Mr Fitton?
Ezra. A lad of nineteen and he doesn't know the elbow game.
(*He rises and moves above the table*) Sit thee down, lad, opposite me.
(*He sits above the table*)

(Eddie *moves and sits* r *of the table*)

Left arm behind. Now take hold of my hand. (*He puts his left arm
behind him and rests his right elbow on the table*) Ready?

(Eddie *grabs Ezra's hand and starts forcing with all his might*)

(*He laughs out loud*) It's like a flea pushing.

(Ezra *puts on the pressure and* Eddie's *hand goes right down. A sudden
gay youthfulness has come over* Ezra)

Eddie. Ee, you are strong, Mr Fitton—where do you get it
from?
Ezra. Forty years of bloody hard work, lad—that's where I get
it from. I'll challenge any of you to the elbow game.
Eddie. Go on, Geoff—have a go with your dad.
Geoffrey. Not likely—look at them maulers, they look like a
couple of number nine shovels.
Ezra. They kept you for many a year, lad.

(Lucy, Liz *and* Molly *enter from the kitchen.* Molly *moves
down* r. Lucy *goes up* c *and* Liz *stands up* r)

Eddie (*rising*) Your Arthur will lick you, Mr Fitton.
Geoffrey. Him! Don't talk daft.
Joe. How could Arthur lick him?
Arthur (*moving to* l *of the table*) What's up now?
Geoffrey. My dad wants to challenge you at the elbow game.
Arthur. I don't feel like taking on any challenges tonight.
Fred. 'Course you don't.
Geoffrey. What, are you chicken?

JOE. He's got enough on his plate.

EDDIE. I bet you could lick him, Arthur.

LIZ. Don't be daft, love, Arthur wouldn't stand a chance with his dad.

EDDIE. He would! I know Arthur's strength—I've wrestled with him.

VIOLET. How do you know he wouldn't have a chance, Mum?

LIZ. He's not got his dad's strength.

VIOLET. Who says he hasn't?

EDDIE. He's got wrists like steel.

EZRA (*rising and looking pointedly at Arthur*) I can't find any challengers.

LUCY. Stop showing off.

(*There is an expectant silence.* LESLIE *and* FRED *move to the fire-place*)

LIZ (*breaking it up*) Well, we'll have to be going now, Leslie. Look at the time. (*She crosses to the clothes pegs* L)

LESLIE. Aye, let's be off.

ARTHUR (*nettled*) Come on, I'll take you on.

LUCY. Now don't be silly, the pair of you.

EZRA. I knew you'd stop him.

ARTHUR (*confident*) I'm not stopping. Come on.

EDDIE. Nobody stops Arthur once he sets his mind on something. You lot are going to get a shock.

(*There are supporting murmurs from either side.* GEOFF, JOE *and* LIZ *support Ezra.* LUCY, VIOLET, MOLLY *and* EDDIE *support Arthur.* EZRA *sits* L *of the table.* ARTHUR *crosses, hangs his jacket on the chair* R *of the table, and sits*)

GEOFFREY (*moving up* L *of the table*) Two-to-one on the old chap.

VIOLET (*moving to* L *of Geoffrey*) I'll take you on.

GEOFFREY. I'll bet you a level half dollar.

EDDIE (*moving behind Arthur's chair*) You've soon brought the odds down.

VIOLET. I'll bet you half a dollar.

EZRA. You'll lose, love.

VIOLET. I won't.

GEOFFREY. Where's your half dollar?

VIOLET (*crossing to Leslie*) Lend me half a crown, Dad. I'll give it to you back after.

LESLIE. Yes, love, but you're backing second favourite. (*He gives Violet half a crown and moves up* R *of the table*)

(VIOLET *crosses and gives the half crown to Geoffrey*)

FRED. A good young 'un'll always lick a good old 'un.

EZRA. Not this old 'un.

GEOFFREY. Here, Fred, you hold the stakes. (*He takes half a crown from his pocket*)

(FRED *crosses to* L *of Geoffrey and takes the coins*)

LUCY (*to Arthur*) Don't bother, love.

GEOFFREY. It's only a bit of fun, Mum. Don't interfere.

LUCY. No good ever comes of any challenges between father and son.

EZRA. Are you frightened I'll lick him?

LUCY (*snorting*) Stop showing off! (*She moves to Molly down* R)

EZRA. Gaah!

(ARTHUR *and* EZRA *face each other and set their elbows on the table*)

What about a referee?

GEOFFREY. I'll be referee.

EZRA. You will hell as like. (*He sweeps Geoffrey away with a sweep of his hand*)

LESLIE. Here, Fred, you be referee.

FRED. Right. Move back. Let the dog see the rabbit.

(FRED *moves above the table and crouches down. The others move in for a better view.* VIOLET *stands up* R *of the table.* LESLIE *stands behind Violet.* JOE *leans over.Fred.* LIZ *stands* L *of Joe.* GEOFFREY *is behind Ezra.* EDDIE *is behind Arthur.* FRED *supervises the position of the elbows and grips*)

ARTHUR. Steady on, you've got my hand gripped tight already.

EZRA. Well, grip mine.

ARTHUR. How can I? It's buried in your mitt. Here, let me take a proper hold.

EZRA. You've got a proper hold.

LUCY. Let go, can't you! Play fair, bighead.

EZRA. D'you mind—non-players off the green.

FRED. Let go, Mr Fitton. Fair's fair. Right, take an even grip. Are you both satisfied?

(ARTHUR *and* EZRA *take a fresh grip*)

EZRA (*to Fred*) Whose side are you on?

FRED. I'm impartial.

EZRA. See as you stay that way.

FRED. What about you, Arthur?

ARTHUR. I'll do.

FRED. Elbows in position? Both ready?

EZRA. Cut the cackle an' let's get on with the contest.

FRED. When I count three you go. One, two, three—*go!*

(*At the word* "*Go*" ARTHUR *starts pressing. He forces* EZRA's *hand down to the table almost at once. There are loud excited cries*)

JOE. That was quick!

EDDIE. He's done it! Arthur's won!

EZRA (*grunting*) Not yet, he hasn't. (*But he is set back*)

LUCY. The lad's won.

FRED (*peering*) His knuckles are not touching the table.

EDDIE. Come on, Arthur.

JOE. It's not over yet.

MOLLY. Just that extra bit, Arthur.

GEOFFREY. Hold on a bit, he's not got it touching. (*He peers over Ezra's chair*)

EDDIE (*yelling*) Go on! Go on! Arthur! What did I tell you.

LESLIE. He's won all right.

GEOFFREY. Hold your water. It's not over yet.

LIZ. Go on, Mr Fitton.

LUCY. He can't. He's licked. Right, big show off!

EZRA (*grunting; riled*) I am hell as like. Watch this.

(*The onlookers go silent as* EZRA *very slowly, with tremendous effort, starts to force* ARTHUR's *arm upwards. He only just does it*)

JOE (*bursting out*) He's getting up. He's rising.

GEOFFREY. Come on, Dad. Come on.

LESLIE. A new favourite.

VIOLET. Shut up, Dad!

EDDIE. Quick, Arthur, force him down again.

(LUCY *and* MOLLY *move behind Arthur*)

GEOFFREY. He can't! He can't! He's only a six furlonger.

EDDIE. Wait for it.

(*They all get very excited as the contest evens up. Finally* EZRA *begins to force* ARTHUR's *hand back. There is renewed shouting*)

VIOLET. Come on, Arthur—don't let him beat you.

EZRA. He can't help it. He's licked and he knows it.

MOLLY. He's not, you know. Not yet. Come on, Arthur.

JOE. He's going red in the face.

EDDIE. He's turning the tables, Mr Fitton.

FRED. Yes, he's coming back.

LUCY. Go on, Arthur, love.

LIZ. Come on, Mr Fitton.

VIOLET. Arthur! Arthur! Arthur!

(ARTHUR *suddenly gains extra strength and forces* EZRA's *hand backwards and downwards. There is a breathless pause, broken by* LUCY *who turns in excitement to Molly*)

LUCY (*with a shout*) Good lad, Arthur. He's won!

EDDIE. Arthur! Come on—come on.

(EZRA, *needled by Lucy's remark, makes a supreme effort. Putting on all his strength he resists the pressure and slowly starts to force* ARTHUR's *arm towards the table*)

FRED (*shouting*) He's not touching.

(*There are more shouts of encouragement from the onlookers as* EZRA *puts on more pressure and finally forces* ARTHUR's *arm down. The knuckles hit the table with a crack.* ARTHUR *lets out a little cry of pain. There are shouts of approval or sympathy, as the case may be*)

EZRA. You're bloody well licked now!

Fred. Aye, here's the winner.
Joe. Father beats son.

(Ezra *holds his son's arm to the table for a moment or two and then rises triumphantly.* Lucy *and* Molly *turn away in disappointment to the fireplace.* Joe *moves up* L, *takes out a gaudy handkerchief and mops his face*)

Geoffrey. Good old Dad, you've licked him. Giss that dollar, Fred.
Fred (*moving to Geoffrey and handing him the coins*) Here y'are. Hard luck, Violet.

(Arthur *rises and puts on his jacket*)

Liz. Three cheers for the winner.
Leslie. Good old Ezra!

(Fred *crosses to the fireplace.* Arthur *goes down* R)

Violet (*moving to* L *of Arthur*) Have you hurt yourself, Arthur?
Arthur. No—it's all right. It's nothing.
Eddie (*moving to* R *of Arthur*) Hard lines, Arthur. I thought once over you had him licked. (*He sits on the left arm of the armchair*)
Violet. So did I.
Ezra (*moving* RC) I told you, didn't I, I could lick you? What do you think of that, Violet? Best man won, eh?

(Violet *tries to comfort* Arthur *but embarrasses him*)

Fred. It was a near thing.
Ezra. It's all that reading he does.
Lucy (*moving to* R *of Ezra*) Shut up! Anyway, look at the size of your hands compared to his.
Ezra (*crossing to* L) I'm twice his age, aren't I? (*Ashamed, but justifying himself*)

(Liz *collects her handbag*)

Fred. It was a good contest. Here, we'd better be going. (*He moves to Arthur and shakes his hand*)

(Ezra *gets a glass of beer and sits on the piano stool*)

Liz. My goodness, it's nearly two o'clock.
Lucy (*crossing to* L) Molly, give me a hand with the coats.

(Ezra *rises.* Molly *crosses to* L *and gets the coats organized.* Fred *shakes hands with Lucy and Ezra.* Eddie *rises and moves up* C. Liz *goes to Violet, kisses her then crosses and gets her coat.* Leslie *crosses to Violet and kisses her. He is very tender with her and this irritates* Liz)

Leslie (*to Violet*) How's my girl? (*He hugs her*)
Violet. I'm all right, Dad. I feel a bit strange like, y'know.
Leslie. The home will seem empty without you, love.
Violet. Don't, Dad—or I'll start crying. You know how I am.
Leslie. Ee, I'm sorry, love. But it will.
Liz (*crossing to* RC; *testily*) Are you two going to stand hugging all night?

VIOLET. What's wrong now, Mum?
LESLIE. I can't hug my own little girl . . .
LIZ. She's not a child any more——
VIOLET (*joking*) You're only jealous, Mum. Eh, Dad? (*She puts her arm around Leslie*) Take no notice.
LIZ. —She's a married woman.
LESLIE. Ee, Liz, I can't imagine it.
VIOLET. Neither can I.
LIZ. Then you'd better start trying—or you'll be in for a shock.

(LESLIE *and* VIOLET *are embarrassed at this frankness, look at each other and turn away*)

(*She turns to Arthur*) Arthur, you two ought to slip off to bed whilst you've chance. Eh, Mrs Fitton?
LUCY. Yes, they ought. There's nothing here for them but beer.

(LIZ *and* LESLIE *cross to* L *and there are "good nights" all round with lots of calls and shouts.*
       LIZ, LESLIE *and* FRED *exit* L. EZRA *starts refilling the glasses*)

EZRA. Come on, chaps.
LUCY. Are you bent on drinking all night?
EZRA. No—only while there's ale in the barrel.

(MOLLY *and* JOE *put on their coats.* GEOFFREY *and* EDDIE *chat up* C. *Attention is diverted from Arthur and Violet.* LUCY *looks quickly around then crosses to* L *of Violet*)

LUCY (*quietly*) Slip off to bed quietly, go on.
VIOLET. Does it not look bad?
LUCY. Does it heck!
ARTHUR. Let's go, Violet.

(LUCY *ushers* VIOLET *and* ARTHUR *up* R *but* JOE *spots them*)

JOE (*moving up* L *of the table*) Aha, are you going to bye-byes?

(MOLLY *knocks* JOE *in the small of the back and he lurches over the table*)

LUCY (*sharply*) Yes, they are—and no funny remarks, Mr Thompson.
JOE. Not me, Mrs Fitton. Good night an' sweet dreams.
GEOFFREY (*crossing to Violet*) Good night, Violet, love. (*He gives her a good kiss*)
JOE. Lay off—you're not the bridegroom.
GEOFFREY. No, but I'm the best man, aren't I?
MOLLY. You'll have Arthur jealous.
ARTHUR. Me? I should want somebody to be jealous of.
VIOLET. Good night, everybody.
JOE (*steadying himself against Geoffrey*) Sleep well. (*He laughs*)
ARTHUR. Good night, all.

(VIOLET *and* ARTHUR *exit up the stairs.* JOE *nudges Geoffrey and Eddie, winks and makes signs about the bed*)

LUCY (*moving to the fireplace*) What's up, Mr. Thompson?
JOE. Nothin' at all. (*To Geoffrey*) Let's get down to some serious drinking. We've got to finish this barrel off. It won't keep.

(MOLLY *gives* JOE *a push and he almost falls.* GEOFFREY *and* EDDIE *get round the barrel.* EZRA *crosses to* RC)

(*To Molly*) Don't push me around—just because you're my wife (*He joins Eddie and Geoffrey at the barrel*)
MOLLY. I married a right Mary Ann I did.

(GEOFFREY, EDDIE *and* JOE *refill their glasses.* JOE *then sits on the piano stool.* GEOFFREY, EDDIE *and* MOLLY *move up* L. LUCY *moves to* R *of Ezra*)

LUCY (*aside to Ezra*) Call yourself a father?
EZRA. What have I done now? (*He is sorry, but covers up*)
LUCY. Did you have to beat the lad like that on his wedding night—in front of Violet and everybody?
EZRA. It was only a game, wasn't it?
LUCY. Would you ha' liked it—if your dad had been there an' licked you in front of everybody on your weddin' night?
EZRA. I tell you it was only a game.
LUCY. You know how the young take these things to heart. Especially our Arthur.
EZRA. Stop pickin' me up over what I do. What counts is what a man feels inside him.
LUCY. How the hell do we know what you feel?
EZRA. You would if you'd let yourself.

(JOE *rises and joins the others up* L)

(*A thought strikes him*) You know as we were struggling there across the table I looked at him and know who he suddenly reminded me of? (*He pauses*) He's even got the same grip. (*He pauses. Sadly*) D'you think I hurt his feelings, Lucy?

(EZRA *and* LUCY *look at each other for a moment with some deeper understanding*)

LUCY (*turning away to the fireplace*) You're always hurtin' 'em.
EZRA. Yet that lad's the last one in the world I'd want to hurt. He's very dear to me. (*He goes up* R, *looks up the stairs, hesitates a moment, then calls*) A right good match, son—hard luck you lost, No ill feeling. Good night.

(*The others have watched curiously. First with humour, half expecting the bed might go, and later with some respect for Arthur's feelings. So for the moment the stage is held with a certain tense atmosphere of curiosity about father and son*)

VIOLET (*off; calling*) Good night. Good night, Mr Fitton.
EZRA (*after a pause*) Good night, love—and God bless. God bless the pair of you. (*He listens for a moment then moves to* R *of the table*)
LUCY. What did he say?
EZRA (*after a pause*) I don't think he answered. It was Violet.

LUCY. I expect the poor lad was too full.

GEOFFREY. You done your best, Dad.

JOE. Aye, you showed willing—no malice.

EDDIE. You don't want to worry, Mr Fitton, Arthur never takes things in bad spirit. He's a good loser.

GEOFFREY. He mustn't have heard you, Dad.

EZRA (*to Lucy*) I try to do right—but somehow it always turns out bloody wrong. (*He sits R of the table*)

LUCY. Yes, and there's a name for a chap as does that.

EZRA. Is there. Then you could call me one.

(*They are all sorry for Ezra.* MOLLY *whispers to Joe and tugs him to the door* L.

GEOFFREY *digs* EDDIE, *who turns and shakes hands with* EZRA, *then he and* GEOFFREY *exit* L.

MOLLY *and* JOE *exit* L. LUCY, *unexpectedly, places a tender, comforting hand on Ezra's shoulder.* EZRA *takes her hand and presses it against his cheek, then rises.*

LUCY *and* EZRA *exit gently up* R, EZRA *switching out the lights as he goes.*

ARTHUR *enters the bedroom, switches on the lights, then stands at the foot of the bed.*

VIOLET *follows him on, closes the door then moves to* L *of Arthur*)

VIOLET. It was nice of your dad to call up.

ARTHUR. Yes—just what I thought.

VIOLET. Why didn't you come and say good night to him?

ARTHUR. I don't know. I wanted to, but when I heard his voice calling I felt I couldn't face him, like.

VIOLET. You all but beat him, you know.

ARTHUR. Somehow I wouldn't want to beat him. Not my own dad.

VIOLET. Yes, I see what you mean.

ARTHUR (*thoughtfully*) He gave me a sudden look.

(*The sound of shunting wagons is heard off.* ARTHUR *crosses to the window and closes it*)

VIOLET. He was the life and soul of the party.

ARTHUR (*thoughtfully*) Yes, he was. I wish I could mix in more. The way he does. He seems rough, but he's got a lovely nature. He was hurt when I didn't have that pint with him. I wish I had now. (*He kisses Violet*) Headache or no headache.

(VIOLET *suddenly sees the roses on the shelves* R)

VIOLET. Oh, Arthur, what lovely roses. (*She crosses to R and picks up the roses*) Are they for me?

ARTHUR. Who else?

(VIOLET *buries her face in the roses*)

VIOLET. Oh, don't they smell wonderful! You think of the nicest things.

ARTHUR (*moving to L of her*) I thought they'd drown the smell of the tannery. It usually comes through the window about this time.

Violet. Don't start worrying—just because you're in your own home. I do love you. (*She puts her arms around Arthur and kisses him*)

(Arthur *responds slowly at the start, but then a passionate urge comes over him and he holds Violet in an intensely loving manner, as though the marriage is about to be consummated on the spot.* Violet *unexpectedly disengages herself, interrupting* Arthur's *mood*)

Here, I'd better put the roses in a vase, hadn't I? (*She goes behind the screen to the washstand, takes the paper off the roses, gets a glass from the shelf, half fills it with water from the carafe and puts the roses in*)

(Arthur *is put out for the moment, but quickly gets over it*)

(*She comes from behind the screen and puts the roses on the dressing-table, then crosses to* R *and looks at a mark on the wall*) What's that line marked "police"?

Arthur. I need to be that height to get in.

Violet. We'll soon stretch that bit out of you.

Arthur. I hope so. I hate working under that Joe Thompson.

Violet. He is a vulgar man. But let's forget 'em all.

Arthur. I only hope my dad doesn't start snoring tonight.

Violet. I've told you to stop worrying.

Arthur. He must sleep with his head against the wall—at times it sets the whole room vibrating.

Violet. You take things too much to heart.

Arthur. He's worse when he's had something to sup. Here, my mum brought you up some water and that—I mean, if you'd like a wash. (*He indicates the washstand behind the screen*)

Violet. Ta very much. How nice of her. (*She removes her shoes and puts them under the dressing-table, then goes behind the screen and removes her dress and stockings*)

Arthur (*calling*) Just call me if there's anything you need.

Violet. It's all right. I think I've got everything.

(Arthur, *with Violet behind the screen and out of sight, begins to pace the room and then decides to sit on the bed. He lowers himself down and just as he is about to rest on it he suddenly springs up as a thought strikes him, turns to speak to Violet and unthinkingly goes behind the screen*)

Arthur. Violet . . .

(Violet *squeals in surprise*)

Oh, sorry. (*He jumps away*) I didn't . . .

Violet (*with an utter absence of coquetry*) It's all right, Arthur. (*She pauses*) I wondered who it was for the minute.

Arthur. I say, would you like some music on whilst you're washing?

Violet. Ee, it's a bit late, isn't it, for music?

Arthur. I'll put it on very low. It's the slow movement from the *Emperor*.

Violet. All right, if you fancy it. They say music soothes the savage beast.

ARTHUR. "Breast", darling. (*He moves to the tape recorder and switches it on*)

VIOLET (*peeping out*) What did you say?

ARTHUR. I said "breast".

VIOLET. Did you?

ARTHUR. Not "beast". "Music hath charms to soothe a savage breast. To soften rocks or bend a knotted oak."

VIOLET. Oh, I see. (*She withdraws behind the screen*)

(*The music commences. It is the second movement of Beethoven's "Emperor". It starts at a point five seconds before the piano comes in. ARTHUR goes to the window, opens it and looks out. The sound is heard of the distant clanging of foundry cranes and industrial night work. ARTHUR closes the window, turns and paces about, humming softly to the tune*)

(*She peeps out*) Arthur, would you pass me my nightie, please?

ARTHUR. Eh? Oh, yes. (*He goes to the bed, picks up the nightdress, looks at it with delicacy, and his mind is taken off the music. He crosses to the screen, hands Violet the nightdress, and kisses her*)

(VIOLET *withdraws behind the screen*)

(*He hums to the music*) Isn't it beautiful!

VIOLET. Yes, it is nice.

ARTHUR. You know what, Violet, there's times when I feel I understand Beethoven better than I do my own dad.

VIOLET. It's only natural. Your dad's in the flesh an' blood, see. You might not understand Beethoven if you lived under the same roof.

(*We now see a sudden change in* ARTHUR. *He is really happy for the first time that evening and his character enlarges before our eyes. He makes us feel that he has found a joy and a content in his own room with his bride. He is confident, likeable and full of a young man's newly-married pride. The Beethoven music adds a certain poignancy to the atmosphere*)

(*With a note of apprehension held down*) I'm nearly ready, Arthur.

ARTHUR (*after a brief pause*) All right, darling. (*He eagerly prepares for bed. He has pushed aside his momentary shyness and now he is a man we can admire. He removes his jacket and tie and hangs them on the back of the chair. He next unties and takes off one shoe and puts it under the chair*)

(VIOLET *shyly emerges from behind the screen, wearing a short nylon nightdress, gay mules on her feet and a short flowery cotton dressing-gown held modestly over her shoulders. She very slowly approaches the bed and stands timidly there*)

(*He looks up from his shoes, sees Violet, approaches her with tenderness and kisses her*) You look so beautiful. (*He holds her harder*) Darling . . . (*He realizes he cannot just stand there*) I'll not be a moment. (*He turns eagerly to undress*)

(*The gown falls from Violet's shoulders to the floor*)

(Violet *quickly picks up her dressing-gown and puts it round herself protectively.* Arthur *sits on the bed to remove his second shoe. The bed promptly collapses with a bang.* Arthur *lets out a cry of astonishment.* Violet *looks dumbfounded and stares down at him*)

Violet. Are you all right, Arthur? (*She laughs hysterically*)

Arthur (*rising*) Shut up! I've had enough laughing for one night.

(Violet *stops laughing*)

(*He switches off the music*) You're just as bad as the bloody rest of them.

Violet *and* Arthur *look at each other. She is shocked at how he has spoken. He is full of anger after this last straw in an evening of setbacks. The bridal pair stare at each other as the lights* Black-Out *and—*

the Curtain *falls*

Scene 2

Scene—*The same. Six weeks later. Night.*
There are slight changes in the furniture. The chair r *has gone and the ottoman is down* c. *The table with the tape-recorder is still down* l.

When the Curtain *rises, the living-room is in darkness. The bedroom is dimly lit by the soft light from the red-shaded bedside lamp.* Arthur, *in pyjamas and looking boyish and helpless, is standing by the open window, smoking a cigarette.* Violet *is asleep in bed. A church clock strikes three. Loud shunting noises are heard. This awakens* Violet. *She turns in bed and sees Arthur by the window. The whole scene is played with a swift, quiet urgency.*

Violet (*sitting up*) Arthur! Arthur, love!

Arthur (*turning nervously and moving* c) Ssh! Ssh! Not so loud, we don't want my mum and dad to hear—or our Geoff.

Violet. Are you standing there again? (*She pauses*) It's been every night alike for weeks. Come back to bed, please.

Arthur. I can't sleep.

Violet. You haven't had one good night's sleep since we got married. What time is it?

Arthur (*sitting on the foot of the bed*) Just gone three.

Violet. I musta fell off.

Arthur. You did.

Violet. Yes, I always do. You'll catch cold standin' there.

Arthur. No, I won't. My skin feels hot like.

Violet. You'd be more comfy here in bed beside me.

Arthur. I get a kind of tingling—just under my skin. I don't know what it is. It makes me feel that I can't rest.

Violet. Get some pills from the doctor to make you sleep.

Arthur. I'd look daft, wouldn't I—only six weeks married and asking for sleeping pills.

VIOLET (*getting out of bed*) I'll go down and make you a cup of tea.

ARTHUR (*rising; sharply*) No, don't. They might hear you. I get a feeling they're listening to us—on both sides.

VIOLET (*sitting on the edge of the bed*) Don't take everything to heart so. You get all tensed up. I can feel you beside me—listening for every sound.

(*Violent shunting sounds are heard off*)

ARTHUR (*moving to the window and closing it*) I had some bloody daft notion that when I got married my life would be transformed. I thought I'd get away from all this lot. And I pictured us in a nice little house on the outskirts of the town——

VIOLET (*rising, crossing to Arthur, and putting her arms around him*) We will, Arthur.

ARTHUR. —Where you'd get the smell of the heather, and the nights would be quiet, and when you looked out you'd see the stars.

VIOLET. Wait till they take you in the police force. They help you to buy your own house.

ARTHUR. They'll never take me. (*He moves* R) Just look at this. (*He stands under the measure against the wall, puts his fingers over his head and then shows them to Violet*) Look.

VIOLET. What's up?

ARTHUR. I'm not getting taller, I'm bloody shrinking.

(*They both laugh and convey a sense of normality beneath their despair*)

VIOLET. It'll come right.

ARTHUR. I feel so sad in my heart—you can't imagine.

VIOLET. Why?

ARTHUR. I've suddenly come to realize that I'll never do any of those things I always imagined I would. It was all a dream.

VIOLET. You will, Arthur. I know you will. You've got more in you than other men.

ARTHUR. It's taking a hell of a time to come out. You mean these books and records? Where have they got me? They've only put ideas in my head that I can't carry out. It's all right whilst I'm reading or listening to music, everything's easy then, but once you've got to go out into the world it's another matter. I sometimes wish I were like my dad—never held a book in my hand. You get a glimpse of another world and it makes you unhappy with your own.

(*There is a pause during which* VIOLET *sits on the left end of the otto-man*)

VIOLET. Are you still worried about the thing we talked over on Sunday night?

ARTHUR. What's that? Oh! Well, yes, in a way. Yes, yes—I am.

VIOLET. I told you to forget all about it.

ARTHUR. It's not that simple for a man. It's been obsessing my mind.

VIOLET. It hasn't made any difference to me. Except I get this feeling you're worrying a lot over it. I'll always love you just the same.

ARTHUR (*with a step towards her*) I can't understand how it could go on all this time.

VIOLET. It'll come right. It's sure to do.

ARTHUR (*crossing and sitting R of Violet on the ottoman*) We said that on the first night, the second—no, not the first—but we did on the second, third, fourth . . .

VIOLET. I can't bear the thought of that first night.

ARTHUR. It was certainly a right bloomin' fiasco. But now it's gone on for six weeks. It's not normal. I know it's not.

VIOLET. Oh, I don't care if it never happens. It's a lot of fuss about nothing if you ask me.

ARTHUR. You wouldn't say that if you were a man. I tell you it's got to happen.

VIOLET. Why? Why has it?

ARTHUR. It has! It must! It's life. This is death, or next door to it.

VIOLET. Don't be daft! We have each other. We love each other. We can still kiss and everything, can't we? I've a feeling that it's because you're obsessed about the other that it doesn't happen.

ARTHUR. It's so bloody frustrating.

VIOLET. And to think I'd such a job holding you back when we were engaged.

ARTHUR. I wish now you'd given way, Vi, if only once. (*He rises, crosses to the dressing-table, takes a cigarette from the packet on it, and lights it*)

VIOLET. I'm not that sort, Arthur. I know it's old-fashioned but I feel we should hold back those special gifts for marriage. You remember last New Year's Eve party?

ARTHUR. Yes, I do for sure.

VIOLET. Do you know I couldn't look my dad in the face when I got home—or my mum, so it was a good job I stopped you when I did. And I've been told a man never respects a girl the same if she lets him be intimate before marriage. (*She rises, crosses to the bed and sits on the edge of it*)

ARTHUR. If you loved a girl you might respect her more. And it would have broken the ice like.

VIOLET. It might have done more. There's always that danger. Then we couldn't have had a white wedding. (*She gets into bed and sits up*)

ARTHUR. We'll be able to have another in a twelvemonth—the way things are going on.

VIOLET. Arthur, I tell you I don't care if it never happens.

ARTHUR. I feel you're only saying that to comfort me. Well, it's damn poor comfort.

VIOLET. I'm not. I mean it. Anyway, what you've never had, you never miss.

ARTHUR. Speak for yourself—I'm not so sure.

VIOLET. Have you no mate you could talk it over with? It might take it off your mind.

ARTHUR. I wouldn't tell a soul. If this got out I'd never hear the end of it. I'd get my leg pulled till kingdom come. Promise you won't ever breathe a word.

VIOLET. Of course I won't. What's it got to do with anybody else?

ARTHUR. I don't know but people always seem interested. That Joe Thompson is always on about it. How long since? He keeps asking. (*He pauses*) Have the girls in the mill not asked you questions?

VIOLET. They've tried—more than once—but I've let 'em see I'm not going to discuss my married life with them.

ARTHUR. I wish there was a bit more to discuss. (*He crosses and sits on the edge of the bed*) Sorry, Vi, for getting so edgy.

VIOLET. 'S all right, Arthur—I understand. It's your nerves.

(ARTHUR *unexpectedly comes out of the mood, puts his arms around Violet and gives her a passionate kiss. The bed gives a loud squeak*)

ARTHUR. Oh, darling, I'm sure it'll come right. I love you so much.

VIOLET. I love you.

(*They kiss passionately. From the next bedroom comes the sound of* EZRA *getting out of bed, yawning and clearing his throat. A light appears through the glass panel of the door, from the next bedroom, where the follow-ing scene is played. The voices are loud and clear*)

(*She breaks from him*) Arthur, I think I can hear your dad getting up.

ARTHUR (*rising and moving to the foot of the bed*) Blast! To hell with him! Curse it!

VIOLET. Arthur! What's up?

ARTHUR (*furiously*) What do you have to bring him up for—just when I was all set? (*He sits on the left end of the ottoman and puts his head in his hands*)

VIOLET. I knew you'd blame it on me.

ARTHUR. Why do you always have to spoil it?

(VIOLET, *near to tears, switches off the bedside lamp*)

VIOLET. I only said I heard him. I know you don't like him hearing us. It's your one fear.

EZRA (*off*) Where is it?

LUCY (*off*) It's under the bed at the bottom. Ssh! Ssh! Hush up —our Arthur and Violet will hear you.

EZRA (*off*) It's coming to something when a man can't answer a call of nature in his own bedroom.

LUCY (*off*) Nature! You mean all that flamin' beer you supped last night.

EZRA (*off*) It's good for the kidneys, isn't it? Why, here it is, round your side.

The lights BLACK-OUT *as—*
the CURTAIN *falls*

Scene 3

SCENE—*The same. The following morning.*

When the CURTAIN *rises, the living-room is lit and the bedroom is in darkness. This scene follows the last very swiftly and is brought in with sounds
of factory buzzers and hooters and other industrial sounds. In the living-
room the remains of breakfast are on the table.* LUCY *is sitting above the
table, pouring tea into a pint mug.* GEOFFREY *is standing* R *of the table,
finishing a mug of tea. He puts down the mug and gets his scarf and leather
jacket from the back of the armchair.*

GEOFFREY. See you later, Mum.

(GEOFFREY *grabs his crash helmet and gloves from the sideboard and
exits to the kitchen*)

(*As he goes*) Ta ra, Dad.

(EZRA *dashes in from the kitchen, wiping his face with a towel*)

EZRA (*calling after Geoffrey*) Ta ra! (*To Lucy*) Has the half past
seven buzzer gone?

LUCY. Yes—this minute. (*She wraps some sandwiches in greaseproof
paper*)

(EZRA *throws the towel over the back of the chair* L *of the table, sits* L
of the table and laces his boots)

(*She rises*) Why do you always throw the towel over the chair?

EZRA. If I did everythin' right, I wouldn't need you—would I?
(*He sips his tea*)

(GEOFFREY *enters from the kitchen, zipping up his jacket*)

GEOFFREY. Tell our Arthur not to forget them complimentary
tickets—I'll take Violet to the pictures tonight.

EZRA. And her husband has to provide the tickets.

GEOFFREY. Why pay for owt that you can get for nowt?

LUCY. You wouldn't take me on a complimentary.

GEOFFREY. I wouldn't take you if they paid me.

LUCY (*giving Geoffrey a playful slap*) Cheeky monkey!

GEOFFREY. Hurry up, Dad—I'll run you to the gasworks on t'back
of my bike.

EZRA. You will 'ell as like! I want to get there in one piece.

GEOFFREY. Windy! So long!

EZRA. So long, lad—God-speed.

LUCY. Be careful, love.

(GEOFFREY *exits cheerfully to the kitchen. A motor-cycle is heard
starting up and driving away*)

EZRA. There's a lad as can look after number one.

LUCY. Aye, most fellas are good at that.

EZRA (*rising*) When is yon chap goin' to get a place of his own?
(*He beckons aloft, then gets his jacket from the chair L and puts it on*)
LUCY. Sh-sh! Don't let them hear you.
EZRA. It's time he heard a bit of truth. I don't feel as the house
is my own.
LUCY. He'll get a place—all in good time.
EZRA. "All in good time." (*He collects his raincoat from the pegs L*)
That's always been your motto. (*He puts his cot on*)
LUCY. Aye, it was my mother's before me. An' her's before her.
(*She stacks the dirty crockery and sets cutlery on the right and left sides of the
table*)
EZRA. He won't if he doesn't stir hissel'. I've told him of two
places—has he gone to see either? Has he hell as like!
LUCY. They weren't nice. The lad's after somethin' better.
EZRA. He's trying to run afore he can walk.
LUCY. He only wants to better himself. He's worried. (*She moves
above the table*)
EZRA. Worried! When I wed you I was gettin' thirty-five bob a
week. What has he to worry about? (*He collects his cap and overalls
from the pegs*)
LUCY. The things that worry folk are not always on the surface.
EZRA (*moving to L of Lucy*) You don't hear young Violet singing
these days like you used to. (*He puts his cap on*)
LUCY. Ee, have you noticed that?
EZRA. She doesn't look you in the eye the same.
LUCY (*glancing towards the door up R*) Sh! I think I can hear her
coming down.
EZRA. The girl's not happy.

(VIOLET *enters up R from the stairs. She is in her dressing-gown and
carries a sponge bag, a towel and some clothes*)

LUCY (*loudly*) 'Morning, Violet love.
VIOLET (*quickly pulling her dressing-gown around her*) Good morning.
Sorry, Mr Fitton, I thought you'd gone.
EZRA. Don't worry, love, I'm just going.

(*The sound of a factory buzzer is heard*)

VIOLET. I'll take my things in the back place. Bye bye, Mr
Fitton.
EZRA. Ta ra, love. Bless you.

(VIOLET *exits to the kitchen*)

LUCY (*to Ezra*) Don't forget your bacon sandwich. (*She picks up
the packet of sandwiches and puts them in Ezra's pocket*) God-speed.
EZRA. She's not happy. (*He moves towards the door up R*)
LUCY. Not that way, Violet's in there. (*She pushes Ezra towards the
front door*) She's got a good husband. (*She goes to the sideboard and takes
a clean handkerchief from the drawer*)
EZRA. I tell you she's not happy.
LUCY (*crossing to Ezra and putting the handkerchief in his pocket*) What

do you expect me to do? I'm pulled one way and another between the lot of you.

EZRA. Just because he's a good son to you doesn't follow he makes a good husband for her.

LUCY. I tell you he's worried because he can't get a home of his own together.

EZRA (*after a pause; unexpectedly*) Lucy, you'll let me know if he needs any cash.

LUCY. I will.

EZRA. I wouldn't like to see the lad short. But don't tell him I offered it. Pretend it's from you. (*He opens the door* L)

LUCY. Go careful. God-speed. Skip the gutter.

> (*There is an odd silent moment of intimacy.*
> EZRA *exits* L)

(*She closes the door, goes to the sideboard, picks up a tray then calls to the kitchen*) Come in, love. He's gone.

> (VIOLET *enters from the kitchen with a towel round her shoulders*)

(*She puts the tray on the table and stacks the dirty crockery on it*) You're up early. I thought you weren't working today.

VIOLET (*moving to* R *of the table*) I'm not. But I thought I'd have a good wash whilst they're out of the way. My dad'll be calling here on his rounds early—an' Arthur didn't sleep so well last night. So I thought I'd let him sleep on.

LUCY. I see. I'll make you some breakfast.

VIOLET. I'm not hungry. Just a cup of tea, please—an' a cream cracker.

> (LUCY *goes round the place tidying up after Ezra and Geoffrey. She is expert at it, shaking things out, folding them, etc.*)

(*She looks upwards and listens*) Is that Arthur getting up?

LUCY. Yes, love. Why?

VIOLET. Don't let him in the back place. Not till I've done.

LUCY. Why not?

VIOLET. Well, I don't think he'd like to see me like this—washing at the sink.

LUCY. More fool him.

VIOLET (*explaining*) It being his own home, like. I won't be long.

LUCY. When you're my age you could parade about in your birth-day suit and they won't give you a second flamin' look.

> (VIOLET *exits to the kitchen.*
> ARTHUR *enters up* R *from the stairs. He is in his dressing-gown*)

ARTHUR. Has he gone? (*He looks around*)

LUCY. Your dad? (*She collects a clean cup and saucer from the sideboard*) He'll be at the gasworks by this.

ARTHUR (*crossing down* L) Where's Violet?

LUCY (*putting the cup and saucer on the table*) Washin' her in the back. (*She moves towards the kitchen*) Will I get you egg an' bacon?

ARTHUR. I don't feel hungry—but I'd like a cup of tea. (*He switches on the transistor radio on the table* L)

(*The music from Mozart's "Eine Kleine Nacht Musik" comes from the radio.* LUCY *gets the teapot from the hearth and pours a cup of tea for Arthur*)

LUCY. When I first wed your dad he could eat a man off a horse for his breakfast.

(ARTHUR *is absorbed in the music*)

(*After a pause*) Oh, our Geoff said not to forget the complimentaries.

ARTHUR (*moving to the table and picking up the cup of tea*) He's generous.

LUCY. There's nothin' wrong between you and Violet?

ARTHUR. Eh? No, why? Has she said anything?

LUCY. No—only your dad was saying he doesn't hear her singin' ·and laughin' like he used to.

ARTHUR. Did he say that? I'd never have thought it.

LUCY. You may not think it, but your dad doesn't miss much.

(ARTHUR *sits on the piano stool* L *and takes a thoughtful drink of tea*)

(*She picks up Ezra's towel and folds it*) That girl needs a home of her own.

ARTHUR (*impatiently; not wanting to talk*) Yes, and so do I. But where can we get one?

LUCY. Not sitting down on your behind listening to music. It won't solve any of your problems.

ARTHUR (*rising abruptly*) I'll go back to bed. (*He puts his cup on the table, picks up the transistor, switches it off and crosses up* R)

LUCY (*putting the towel on the sideboard*) You're a good lad, love, but you are inclined to bottle up your feelings.

ARTHUR. What about if I do?

LUCY. One day they might bottle you up. I know, it once happened to me. They've got to come out one way or another.

ARTHUR. It'll be all right, Mum.

(*There is a sudden, deep, intuitive silence between* MOTHER *and* SON. ARTHUR *turns to go, then prompted by something in Lucy's words, he turns, hesitates, then gives her a shy, comforting kiss.* LUCY *gives him a quick, clumsy hug, full of feeling.*
ARTHUR *gives her a "Cheer up, Mum," pat on the shoulder and exits hurriedly up* R *to the stairs.* LUCY *looks after him. For a long moment she stands there, staring silently in front of her, then she takes the hem of her apron to wipe her eyes, trying to force back her tears.*
VIOLET *enters from the kitchen wearing an attractive housecoat and looking very pretty. She carries her towel and sponge bag*)

VIOLET (*as she enters*) Where's Arthur? (*She stops, disappointed*)

(LUCY *dabs her eyes*)

(*She goes to Lucy. Tenderly*) Is everything all right?

(LUCY *nods quickly, wipes her eyes, moves to the table and finishes stacking the crockery*)

LUCY. Life's funny, love.

(VIOLET *moves to* R *of Lucy*)

He's just gone back to bed. (*She looks closely at Violet*) There's nothing wrong between you an' him, is there, love?

(VIOLET *turns guiltily away and hangs her towel and sponge bag on the chair* R *of the table*)

VIOLET. No—why—has he said anything?

(*The Mozart music from the transistor is heard off upstairs*)

LUCY. I just wondered. Why don't you make a fresh pot of coffee and take it up, just for the two of you?

VIOLET. Do you think he'd like it?

LUCY. He'd love it. (*She looks upwards*) He wants his mind takin' off that for a bit. (*She moves to the pegs* L *and takes down her coat*)

(VIOLET *crosses and helps* LUCY *to put on her coat*)

Where's my basket? (*She collects her basket from the corner up* L) I'll not be back for a bit, love. (*She unexpectedly hugs and kisses Violet*) I've a few errands to do. Make that coffee.

(LUCY *exits by the street door.* VIOLET *realizes this is her chance. She goes to the table, puts the milk and sugar on the tray and carries the load of dirty crockery off to the kitchen. She re-enters with a small tray with a basin of sugar and two apples. She puts the tray on the table and begins to prepare herself. She takes a brush, comb and a scent spray from her sponge bag, moves to the fireplace, looks in the mirror, and tidies her hair. She puts on some scent, this is an elaborate performance. She arranges her housecoat so that her bust looks more interesting. She hums to the music. The sound of a kettle whistling is heard from the kitchen.*

VIOLET *replaces the brush, etc., in the sponge bag and exits to the kitchen. She re-enters with two cups of coffee and some toast and puts them on the tray. She gives the final touches to the tray, then to herself. The music continues from the bedroom. She is ready. She picks up the tray and moves to the stairs. Suddenly there is a sharp knocking at the street door.* VIOLET *does not quite know what to do. She is set back. She decides to go upstairs. There is a second knock. She puts the tray on the table, crosses to the street door and opens it.*

LIZ *is outside the door*)

LIZ. Hello, love. Has your dad been round yet?

VIOLET. Ee, hullo. No. Why? (*She stands aside*)

(LIZ *comes into the room and crosses to* L *of the table*)

LIZ. Ee, I'm glad I've not missed him. Harry Taylor brought a death certificate round—the old gran snuffed it at last. (*She holds out the book and certificate*)

(VIOLET *closes the door, takes the book and certificate and puts them on the sideboard*)

So if you see your dad gets it when he calls, oh, an' tell him they'll want about fifty quid to be goin' on with.

VIOLET (*moving up* R *of the table*) All right, Mum. (*She hopes she might get rid of Liz*) I'll tell him.

LIZ. Oh, that's all right, then, isn't it? Where's Mrs Fitton?

VIOLET. Gone off somewhere.

LIZ. Is there only you and Arthur at home?

VIOLET. Yes. (*She pauses*) I was just taking him some coffee and toast up.

LIZ. Oh, coffee, eh? Smells nice.

VIOLET (*desperate*) Would you like a cup?

LIZ. I wouldn't say no if I were offered one. (*She looks at the tray*) Two cups?

VIOLET. I thought I'd have one with him.

LIZ. Eee, I'll go, then.

VIOLET. No—don't, Mum.

LIZ. Ee—I don't want to interrupt anything.

VIOLET. You're not. I promise you.

LIZ. No, love—I won't take away your married pleasure.

VIOLET. What pleasure?

LIZ. There's precious little of it when you get to my age.

VIOLET. Sit down, Mum, and have a cup of coffee. (*She sits* R *of the table*)

(*The music ceases*)

LIZ. Thank heaven. That din was getting on my nerves. (*She sits above the table*) Do you mind if I smoke? (*She takes cigarettes and matches from her handbag*)

VIOLET. 'Course I don't.

(LIZ *lights a cigarette*)

What were you saying, Mum?

LIZ. I don't like to see a woman smokin'—but it eases my nerves. Never mind about me—are you feelin' all right, love?

VIOLET. 'Course I am—why?

LIZ. I thought you looked tired when I came in. "She's not gettin' enough sleep," I says to myself, "but I suppose it's only what you can expect." (*She looks around*) Any word about a place of your own, yet?

VIOLET (*handing a cup of coffee to Liz*) No—but we keep living in hope.

LIZ. You want to be careful, you know.

VIOLET. How do you mean—"careful"?

LIZ. Careful as you don't start something before you've got a place of your own.

VIOLET. Oh, do you mean a baby?

LIZ. What else can you start?

Violet. We won't.

Liz. You young wives are all the same. Florrie Anderson wouldn't stand being told—seven months later she landed herself with twins. She were going by the pill method.

Violet. Well, it won't happen to us.

Liz. You can go by what method you want, her gran told her. Nature will find a way through. It always has done—it always will. That's what it's there for.

Violet. It'll have a job in our case.

Liz (*huffily*) I think I'll be off. (*She rises and stubs out her cigarette in the ashtray on the table*) Married six weeks and she knows more than her own mother. (*She moves to the street door*)

Violet (*rising and moving above the table*) Don't go, Mum, please. All I meant was that you don't have to warn me about having a baby too soon.

Liz (*knowingly*) Why? (*She moves to L of Violet*) What's different about you from anybody else? Eh? (*She looks Violet up and down*)

Violet. Oh, nothing—nothing at all.

Liz. Why will it have a job in your case? Out with it.

(Violet *hesitates, turns away and sits above the table*)

Violet. You won't say anything to anybody, will you, Mummy?

(Liz, *all alert, pulls the chair L of the table to L of Violet and sits*)

Liz (*eager to hear the news*) Of course I won't love. What have you to tell me? Go on—I'm your mother. Don't be shy.

Violet (*turning to her*) Nothing's happened yet—you know— that could make me like that.

Liz. Eh? Nothing's happened? You don't mean—d'you—you can't mean that . . .

Violet. I mean—y'know—things are just the same, like.

Liz. You don't mean Arthur hasn't . . . ?

Violet. No—yes—I mean—y'know—like.

Liz. You mean he hasn't got round to it yet?

Violet. No—not properly.

Liz. Good grief—you mean not even once?

Violet. No—no—I don't think so.

Liz (*loudly*) What do you mean—"don't think so"?

Violet (*rising and moving up* R) Sh—sh—not so loud. I swore I wouldn't breathe a word. (*She closes the curtain up* R)

Liz. He either has—or he hasn't.

Violet. Don't cross-examine me. I've told you, haven't I? I'm not going into details.

Liz. Ee, fancy, you haven't brought it off. So you're still a vir . . . Are you?

Violet. 'Course I am.

Liz (*staring at Violet*) I just wondered.

Violet (*moving to the fireplace*) Don't stare at me like that, Mummy. I don't want your pity.

Liz. The look slipped out, love. Ee, but this is a shock.

VIOLET (*turning*) Why—it's not all that serious, Mummy—is it?

LIZ. It could ruin your whole married life—your health—your nerves—everything.

VIOLET (*after a pause*) I don't believe you. (*Weakly*) How could it?

LIZ. I don't know, love—but it could. It don't mean no more than that—(*she snaps her fingers*) if you do it—but by heck if you don't, it builds up. Nothing's worse. *I* know. (*She rises and crosses to* L *of Violet*) You haven't told anybody, have you?

VIOLET. Ooh, no—I wouldn't dream of mentioning our private life . . .

LIZ. It 'ud be a right scandal, all over the town if it got out. Everybody yakity-yak!

VIOLET. But why? Why? A private thing like that.

LIZ. Don't ask why—believe me, it just would. The more private a thing is the more they gossip. Folk 'ud look on you as lepers. It's what lies behind it, do you follow me?

VIOLET. Nothing lies behind it. Don't let us talk about it any more.

LIZ. We've got to thrash it out.

VIOLET. I can't see anything wrong in it.

LIZ. It's how it strikes the mind. Folks would call it unnatural. (*She pauses and moves below the table*) Do you know you're not properly married till . . .

VIOLET (*with a step towards Liz*) That's not true!

LIZ (*moving to* L *of Violet*) Ee, I wouldn't tell you a lie. Cath'lics can't have a divorce—but if that hasn't happened they just annul the marriage. I know it looks nothing to you, love, in your innocence, but there's so much behind it. (*She points upwards*) He's not a proper husband yet—an' you're not a proper wife.

VIOLET (*moving down* R *and putting her hands over her ears; with an outburst*) Don't—don't say that! I won't listen.

LIZ (*following her*) It's true. You're married in name only.

VIOLET. Stop it! Stop it! (*Utterly shocked*) I wish I'd never told you! How can you say a thing like that? (*She sobs loudly*)

(*There is a light knock on the street door*)

LIZ. Hush up! Somebody's coming.

(VIOLET *moves quickly, picks up the tray of coffee and exits to the kitchen.*

    LESLIE *opens the street door and enters. He is bright and brisk and carries an attache case*)

LESLIE (*coming into the room and removing his hat; happily*) It's only me. (*His face falls as he sees Liz*) Oh—you're here! (*He puts his case and hat on the table. He senses the atmosphere*) I say—what's up? What's wrong? (*He moves down* LC)

LIZ. Just wait till you hear.

(VIOLET *enters from the kitchen and rushes, sobbing, into* LESLIE'S *arms*)

Violet. Oh, Dad! Dad! Dad!

Liz. No use turning to your dad—he can't help you this time.

(Leslie, *upset, comforts Violet*)

Leslie (*turning to Liz*) What's wrong with the child?

Liz. Ask her. Ask your little girl.

Violet. She says I'm not a proper wife. Oh, Dad—take me home —I'm so unhappy—I want to go back home.

Violet *sobs as—*

the Curtain *falls*

ACT II

Scene 1

Scene—*The same. The evening of the same day.*

When the Curtain *rises, the lights and the fire are on in the living-room and the bedroom is in darkness. In the living-room,* Ezra, *seated above the table, is concentrating on the task of polishing up an old cornet. He is well-washed and wears old but clean trousers and shirt, slippers, braces and a thick leather belt.* Lucy, *bored, is seated in the armchair with one of Ezra's working shirts on her knee, which she is mending. There is a long silence.*

Lucy. Shouldn't they have brought the telly back today?
Ezra. I don't care if they never bring it back.

(*There is a long silence*)

That thing were killing the art of conversation in the home.
Lucy (*after a pause*) I see what you mean.
Ezra (*looking admiringly at the cornet*) Remember how I could play it years ago, Lucy?
Lucy. There's a shop in town pays a good price for old instruments.
Ezra. Oh, aye—well, I'd never think of selling this'n. It's not mine by rights: you know who left it here. I used to love to hear him play. He had a beautiful lip.

(Lucy *looks thoughtful.* Ezra *puts the cornet to his lips and plays "I'll Send Thee Red, Red Roses". There is a knock at the street door.* Lucy *rises, goes to Ezra and taps him on the shoulder.* Ezra *stops playing*)

Lucy. There's somebody at the door.
Ezra. Eh? Blast! Don't ask 'em in.
Lucy. I won't—if I can help it. (*She goes to the street door and opens it*) Ee, Mr and Mrs Piper—fancy. Come in, will ya?

(Ezra *looks put out. He jumps up and guiltily hides the cornet up* R.
Liz *and* Leslie, *looking gloomy, enter by the street door*)

Leslie. Hello, there.
Ezra (*moving up* R *of the table*) How go. What a pleasant surprise.
Liz (*crossing to the armchair*) I hope we haven't disturbed you.
Ezra. Ee, no—not at all. Take us as you find us.
Lucy (*closing the door and moving to* L *of Ezra*) What's seldom's wonderful. Sit down.
Liz. Thank you. (*She gives Leslie a look and sits in the armchair*)
Leslie (*after a pause*) You are alone? I mean, nobody else in the house?

Lucy. Our Geoff's taken your Violet to the pictures. An' of course, our Arthur's workin'.

Leslie. Good. (*He sits* l *of the table*)

Liz. We were bankin' on you being **alone.**

Lucy. Oh . . .

Ezra. Put the kettle on, Lucy.

Liz. We've just this minute finished **our tea.**

Lucy. Are you sure?

Leslie. Positive.

Lucy. It's no trouble.

Liz. Not just now, thanks.

Ezra. Put it on, Lucy.

Lucy. You 'eard 'em say they **didn't want any.**

Leslie. No, definitely not.

Liz. Thanks very much all **the same.**

(*There is a silence*)

Ezra. It's manners to refuse, isn't it? They might be **thirsty.**

(Lucy *gives* Ezra *a look and he shuts up*)

Leslie. We just had our tea.

Liz. I expect you must be wonderin' what brought us **round.** Shall I go on, Leslie, or will you?

Leslie. You—you've got it all off.

Ezra. Is there owt wrong?

Leslie. Wait till you hear, Mrs Fitton.

Liz. That's why I thought we should call a shop meeting, **like,** to talk it over.

Lucy. To talk what over?

Liz. You know I called round this morning.

Lucy. That's right.

Liz. Well, I'd an intimate chat with our Violet, and it came out by chance. Didn't you know?

Ezra. Know what?

Liz (*to Leslie*) I told you they couldn't have known, Leslie, or they'd come over to us.

(Ezra *and* Lucy *exchange one of their rare looks*)

Ezra. What about?

Leslie. Our Violet cried in my arms. She wanted to come back.

Liz. It was only nerves. It's got to be faced. The girl's got pluck. She'll stick it out whilst there's a ray of hope.

Ezra. Stick what out?

Liz. It's about their marriage. Would you like to take over from there, Leslie?

Leslie. No, carry on—same as I say, you have it all off.

Lucy. Now what about their marriage?

Liz. It hasn't taken on yet—if you see what I mean. Y'know.

Lucy. Ee, get off—you don't mean . . . ? Nay, that can't be true.

Liz. Just what I said.

Leslie. But it seems it is.

Lucy (*sitting above the table*) Well, I never. That explains a lot. No wonder they haven't been sleeping well.

Liz (*with a telling glance at Leslie*) If it's not one thing keeping a body awake, it's another.

Ezra (*bewildered*) Taken on? Taken on what?

Lucy. They haven't taken the plunge yet—you nit. Well, well, well, no wonder they didn't want no breakfast.

Ezra (*mystified*) What plunge? (*He looks at Liz*)

Lucy. What do you think?

Leslie. There's only one plunge, as far as I know.

Lucy. He wants to know everything—but he still knows nothing.

Liz. Their marriage hasn't found itself yet, Mr Fitton.

Lucy (*after a pause*) He's still not with it.

Leslie. In other words, it hasn't gelled.

(Ezra *looks from one to another*)

Ezra. Gelled? How do you mean?

Liz. Our Violet's still as if she were a single girl, Mr Fitton. (*She pauses*) She's still intact.

Lucy. Intact. A virgin, if you like. Now have you got it?

Liz. Thank you, Mrs Fitton.

Ezra. Do you mean to say . . . ?

Leslie. She means what she says, Mr Fitton.

Ezra. Does that mean our Arthur hasn't . . . ?

Leslie. No, he hasn't.

Liz. It seems he hasn't gone about it properly.

Lucy. It seems neither of 'em has.

Ezra. You mean they haven't . . . ?

Lucy. No, they haven't.

Ezra (*looking nonplussed*) Get off—after six weeks. (*In wonderment*) Well, well!

Lucy. It's taken the penny long enough to drop. (*To Liz*) Was she certain?

Liz. At the start she tried to make out she wasn't sure but I fancy that was only a hint there had been something.

Lucy. Oh, there's bound to have been *some* overture—but if the main item had been performed she'd have been left in no doubt.

(Ezra *is embarrassed*)

Leslie. Let's try to keep to the point.

(Liz *and* Lucy *exchange looks*)

Ezra (*helplessly*) Can it be possible, Lucy?

Lucy. You don't want a doctor's certificate, d'you? (*To Liz*) She didn't give you any details?

Liz (*rising*) Eh? Details? There wouldn't be any, would there?

Ezra (*crossing and sitting on the stool down* R) Well, I don't know what to say.

Lucy. In that case, you'd better keep your mouth shut.

Liz (*sitting* r *of the table*) I understand how Mr Fitton must feel —being Arthur's father.

Lucy. Well, I'm glad somebody understands him—it's more than I've ever been able to. (*To Ezra*) Anyway, why should you get so het up?

Ezra. Think of the disgrace.

Lucy. What disgrace?

Ezra. Suppose it leaked out at the gasworks, eh?

(Liz *cackles*)

Liz. Excuse me . . .

Lucy. Who the hell cares about the flamin' old gasworks?

Ezra (*rising and crossing to* r *of Lucy; with conviction*) I do. An' why shouldn't I? I've worked there for twenty-nine years. I want to go on working there. But if this got out, I'd never be able to live it down. I couldn't face my mates of a morning. (*He sits in the armchair*) I'd go and drown my bloody self, I would—to think a son of mine can't prove his manhood.

Lucy. Oh, is that how you prove it? Fancy that!

Liz. What are we going to do—that's the question.

Leslie. Aye, an' it'll take a bit of answering.

Lucy. Well, you can't hold a gun to folks' heads and tell 'em to get started.

Ezra (*pained*) Lucy!

Lucy (*mimicking*) "Lucy!" Knowing our Arthur—and your Violet, I've a strong feeling they'll come to their cake and milk all in good time.

Ezra. If he hasn't come to it in six bloomin' weeks—an' it there beside him—I doubt if he'll ever come to it.

Liz (*emphatically*) Yes, let's face it, the longer a man goes without working up to it the less inclined he is to start. (*She is speaking from experience*) It's an instinct—and an instinct is nothing if it isn't working. (*She glances at Leslie*) You don't get husbands doing that sort of thing out of pity.

Lucy. Not likely. Pleasure or nothing for the man.

Leslie. Let's not get personal.

Liz. I know how they hate facing up to things in case their own particular weaknesses comes out.

Lucy (*glancing at Leslie*) I see what you mean. Now, what had you in mind, Mrs Piper?

Liz. I'll have another talk with our Violet.

Leslie. Look, I think I'm entitled to . . .

Liz. All right, Leslie. I'll deal with this. Now, I'll have a good talk with our Violet to see if I can find out what's causing the obstruction. Now, will you take Arthur on one side, Mr Fitton, and have a talk with him?

Ezra. Who? Me? But I've never had a proper talk with the lad in all my life.

Lucy. A nice thing for a father to say.

EZRA. You never know what to say to 'em these days. Anyway, he always seems to be grinning to himself every time I say anything to him.

LUCY. Doesn't know what to say to his own son.

EZRA (*desperately*) What is there to say about *that* as 'ud be of any use, Mr Piper?

LESLIE. The only thing for him to do is to go blind at it same as everybody else has to.

LUCY. Our Arthur never goes blind at anything. He's not that way inclined.

EZRA. Why don't you talk to him? Eh? You're as thick as thieves.

LUCY. It's not a mother's duty.

EZRA. He turns to you—but does he ever turn to me?

LUCY. He feels you don't understand him—and that you don't want to understand him. Anyway, I never knew it worried you.

EZRA. I don't let it. But I feel it. I'm human, y'know.

LESLIE (*avoiding Liz's eye*) It's only natural for a son to turn to his mother, like a daughter will to her dad.

(LIZ *gives Leslie a look*)

EZRA. Turning is one thing—but I hate to see a "mammy's boy".

LUCY. He's no mammy's boy—but if a lad can't love his own mother, then he can't love anybody, because that's where love starts, at the breast.

EZRA (*rising; pained*) I wish you wouldn't use words like breast when we've company. (*He picks up the cornet and rubs it with embarrassment*)

LUCY. Harken him! Bloody bottle fed—his mother told me the milk had run out when he arrived on the scene.

EZRA. It's word I'd never use in mixed company.

LUCY (*shouting*) Say "pap" and have done with it.

EZRA. Lucy! (*He turns away and replaces the cornet*)

LUCY. I told you he were bottle fed.

LESLIE. Has your Arthur ever knocked about much with girls?

LUCY. No—he's not a knocker-abouter. When he got home from his work at the pictures he liked to go to his room and listen to his record player.

EZRA (*in an outburst; fuming and embarrassed*) That bloody chamber music is behind all this. I can feel it in my bones. (*He sits in the armchair*)

LUCY. Shut up about his music.

EZRA. I will not. He turns that flamin' din on and he shuts his mind against life. He were never brought up to it.

LUCY. No marriage goes off with a bang from the start but folk don't like admitting it. I'm talking from experience.

EZRA. Y'what?

LUCY. I said I was talking from experience.

Ezra. Well, I might be no Romeo but there's nowt odd or queer about me—not like some folk.

(*An unexpected quietness drops into the atmosphere*)

Lucy. What do you mean by that? (*She knows*)

Ezra. What I say.

Lucy. What have you got behind your mind?

Ezra (*rising and moving to* R *of Lucy; shouting*) That bloody son of yours has shamed me—I can hardly bear to stand here. All his fancy music, fancy readin' and fancy bloody talk, an' when it comes to it he can't fulfil his married duties. There's something very odd, very queer about that lot. (*He turns away to the fireplace and fiddles with his pipe*)

Lucy (*after a long pause; reflectively*) Would you say there was anything odd or queer about a chap who went on his honeymoon and took his mate with him?

(Ezra *gives a slight turn of the head*)

Liz. A mate? You don't mean another man—a pal? (*With a short laugh*) I'd say that was a rum carry-on.

Leslie. What would you want your chum for on your honeymoon? (*He laughs*)

Ezra (*turning*) Are you referring to me?

(Leslie *and* Liz *react with surprise*)

Lucy. Who else? You're the only chap I know who's done it.

Ezra. But I didn't *take* him on the honeymoon, Lucy.

Lucy. All right, you didn't *take* him. But we all three travelled on the same train to Blackpool, didn't we? In the same compartment—you two sat next to one another, laughin' your heads off.

Ezra (*mildly and reasonably*) But we'd had a bit to drink, Lucy—and that was only how we *went* on our honeymoon.

Lucy (*to Liz*) Then at Blackpool we all three got out of the train and got into a cab together.

Ezra (*hurt*) But, Lucy, you didn't want for Billy to get a cab on his own, did you?

Lucy (*to Liz*) Then we all three went trooping into the same boarding-house together—*Honeymoon Villa.*

Ezra (*moving to* R *of Lucy*) But, Lucy, you didn't expect me to tell Billy to go off and find a room on his own—a lad who'd never set foot in a boarding-house in his life.

Lucy. Then at night we all three went off dancing at the *Tower* together.

Ezra. But you don't mean we should have left Billy behind, do you, Lucy? A shy lad all alone in Blackpool. As I recall we made a happy little trio strolling along the promenade.

Lucy (*to Liz*) I had to have one dance with my husband, and then one with his mate, then . . .

Ezra. What else, Lucy? Share an' share alike.

Lucy. Then the next dance they'd have together.

LESLIE. You what?

LIZ. Get off!

(LESLIE *and* LIZ *look at Ezra*)

LUCY. Yes—standing up against the bar side by side suppin' pints of ale.

EZRA. But, Lucy, I couldn't ask Billy to go an' drink on his own.

LIZ. But, Mr Fitton, you were on your honeymoon.

EZRA. Aye, I know—but I'm only human. A chap can't change his nature overnight—just because he's gone an' got wed.

LESLIE. Aren't we gettin' off the subject?

LIZ (*aside to Leslie*) Keep your mouth shut, can't you?

LUCY. Then we came back and sat down to our supper together.

EZRA (*reproachfully*) But, Lucy—did you want for Billy to go an' sit at a table all by himself? The food woulda bloody choked me at the thought of it. You didn't marry a savage, y'know. He had his bedroom an' we had ours. What more do you want? (*He sits on the stool down* R)

LUCY. You talking about things looking odd—well, I'm only saying as that looked odd—to see two men and one woman sittin' down to breakfast every mornin' at the honeymoon table by the window.

EZRA. What was odd about it? Anyway, me an' Billy had already been for our morning walk along the front, don't forget.

LUCY. I'm not likely to. D'you know, every morning that honeymoon week he'd jump out of bed as the church clock struck the first note of seven.

LESLIE. That's an early rise for a honeymoon.

EZRA. I couldn't ask him into our bedroom, Lucy—you know how embarrassed he would have been.

LIZ (*to Lucy*) Was that before they'd brought you round the morning tea?

LUCY. Tea! No sign of tea. He was the first up in the place. The next thing I'd hear this funny little whistle outside our bedroom door. (*She whistles*) Then off my husband 'ud scamper like a lad going fishing—without so much as a good-bye kiss.

EZRA. I never was one to take liberties with other folks' bodies.

LIZ. But, Mr Fitton, she was your wife.

EZRA. Aye, I know—but you can still show a bit of respect—you don't own a woman just because you've wed her. Kiss your wife in bed of a morning. What a liberty to take with a young girl.

LIZ. But you'd slept beside her all night, Mr Fitton.

EZRA. I slept beside my brother Tom for years—but I never damn well kissed him. An' what a chap does in the dark is one thing —an' what he'll do in the daylight is quite another.

LUCY. Then I'd hear their feet striding along the pavement— and I'd jump out of bed and watch them from behind the curtain.

EZRA. Whatever for, Lucy?

LUCY. Because I was a damn fool, I expect. An' I'd see 'em both making for the sea—shoulders back, chests out.

EZRA. Could you blame us? That sea air tasted lovely after a twelve-month at the gasworks. Happy days. (*With a sudden change of mood as a happy memory comes back*) Lucy, remember them new brown shoes me an' Billy bought ourselves for the honeymoon?

LUCY. Your officer's field boots as you called 'em. (*To Liz*) He used to spend half an hour of spit an' polish on 'em every night before he came to bed.

EZRA (*rising*) What smooth fine leather, came up over the ankles, the only decent pair of shoon I'd had in my life. I remember the first Sunday morning, Lucy—me an' Billy went for our walk along the sea front, we strolled across the sands and stood there right at the edge of the sea, when suddenly a little frothy ripple of tide comes in an' rolls clean over our new brown shoon. An' when I looked down I saw it roll off like water off a duck's back—they were that well polished, see. An' then I sees on top of my new brown shoon all these shining drops of sea water glistening away. I'll never forget it. *That* was the big moment of my honeymoon.

LIZ. The *big* moment, Mr Fitton?

EZRA. Big or little—it were a moment of beauty. There aren't that many in life as you can afford to forget 'em. Eh, Mr Piper?

LESLIE (*sadly*) I've forgotten any I ever had.

LUCY. Then you both came back in your new brown shoon an' sat one either side of me—for breakfast.

EZRA. What was wrong about it, Lucy?

LUCY. I don't know. But whichever way you look at a honeymoon for three, and there's more than one way you can look at it, it musta seemed damned queer to them folk as were sittin' there, watchin' us. (*To Liz*) Why, I didn't know how to face them.

LIZ. Aye, times two's company an' three's a crowd.

LESLIE. Aren't we . . . ?

(LIZ *looks at Leslie*)

LUCY. I never knew which way to look. I could see folk starin' at us.

EZRA. I wish I'd have known. I'd have given 'em something to bloody stare at. (*He pauses*) It's twenty-eight years since all that happened, Lucy, and this is the first time you've ever broached it.

LUCY (*after a pause*) Well, you drew it out of me. (*She rises and turns away up* c) The lad's no more odd or queer than you an' Billy were. An' even if he had have been—Nature would ha' done it, an' Nature is not to be thwarted. An' it's a father's duty to help an' protect a lad like that—since it must come through the father or the mother—not to turn on him like the mob would, an' tear his self-respect to ribbons, all over somethin' he had no say in.

EZRA (*after a pause; quietly*) You know I'd never turn on the lad, Lucy, if he needed me.

LIZ. Now, there's no need to get upset, Mrs Fitton, since we all know Arthur's quite normal.

LUCY. Yes, but I thought I'd let him see what it feels like to be suspected. We all have a weak spot somewhere.

LESLIE (*after a pause*) What happened to him?
EZRA. Who?
LIZ. Y'know—Billy.
EZRA. Eh? Billy. Oh, I doubt you'd like somethin' to sup. I'll
slip out to the off-licence. Lucy, did we have one cross word that
week at Blackpool? Or was there ever any hard words or quarrelling
in our home during Billy's day?
LUCY. No, I don't think so. Why? (*She takes a jug from the side-
board cupboard*)
EZRA (*moving to Lucy*) You see, Lucy, I came across a new feeling
of happiness that week, so what more natural in a man that he
should want to spread it, and make his best friend happy, too?
LUCY. Here y'are. (*She hands the jug to Ezra*)
EZRA (*crossing to the street door*) I do realize now that it can never
quite work out that way. (*To the Pipers*) Sorry, I'll not be long.
LESLIE. But what about Billy?
EZRA. Billy? Ask Lucy there, she saw him last.

(EZRA *exits to the street.* LUCY *takes a glass cloth from the sideboard
drawer, and four glasses from the sideboard cupboard*)

LUCY (*putting the glasses on the table*) He used to come round every
evening when we were first married. (*She polishes the glasses*) He were
very good with his hands and made us shelves and cupboards, and
I got used to him and Ezra talkin' away and coddin' each other like
two school lads. Then he came round one evening in May when I
was white-washin' the back bedroom and Ezra was working late.
So whilst he was waiting I asked him to come up an' hold the
ladder for me. It was one of those very warm evenings you sometimes
get in May with a warm breeze that they say comes from Africa.
There was Billy holding the ladder. I kept splashin' him and laughin'
—I must have had a funny mood on me. I was only a girl, you could
say, nineteen—you know how you are. But Billy wasn't laughing.
I enjoyed it all the more—to see him gettin' worked up like. And
him being a shy lad at heart. I remember it like it was only this
afternoon.
LIZ (*after a long pause*) Yes? Go on, what happened?
LUCY (*absent-mindedly polishing*) Y'what?
LESLIE. You were doin' the back bedroom with Billy.
LUCY (*coming out of her daze*) He didn't stay on and wait for Ezra
that night. He went off before Ezra came home. Ezra couldn't make
it out. And he didn't come round the night after, nor the night
after that—do you know, I've never seen him from that day to this.
LESLIE. And didn't Ezra go and seek him out?
LUCY. He wanted to but I wouldn't let him. I've often been sorry
since, but at the time I had to do it. With the woman the home
comes first—not friendship. Eee, but I can't tell you how empty
our little house was on those evenings—without him.
LIZ. I expect you both had him on your minds.
LUCY. In a way. Then Billy went down South to work at one of
them motor car factories. It near broke Ezra's heart. 'Course it

must have been around then I started off with our Arthur, so I had something to occupy my mind—and it was God's blessing when he were born, and Ezra had someone to come home to—the child, see, to take Billy's place like. In some way he reminds me of Billy—he's got the same smile an' takes things to heart just the same. Eee, but he were a lovely lad.

(EZRA *enters from the street, carrying a jug of beer and two small bottles of stout*)

You've not been long.

EZRA (*putting the jug and bottles on the table*) I got served quick. (*He points to the jug*) Draught beer. You can't beat it. The bottle stuff always fills me with wind. (*He takes two more bottles of stout from his pockets and puts them on the table*) I fetched some bottled stout for the ladies.

LIZ. It doesn't matter about us having the wind.

(LUCY *pours two glasses of stout and hands one to Liz*)

EZRA (*pouring two glasses of beer from the jug*) Ladies can handle it better. (*He hands a glass of beer to Leslie*)

(*There is laughter and relief.* EZRA *and* LUCY *clink glasses before they drink then* EZRA *crosses and sits in the armchair. There is a pause. The atmosphere is more friendly*)

LESLIE. Now, about your Arthur again . . .

LIZ. Listen—I think I've got this job beat. You know what our Violet can do—tomorrow being Saturday she could go and talk it over with her Uncle Fred. You know—him who was at the wedding.

(*Drinking never really starts*)

LUCY (*sitting above the table*) Yes, he's a nice man.

LESLIE. Why—what could he do?

LIZ. He could advise her. He's a physiotherapist. He's had more bodies under his hands than you've had breakfasts.

EZRA (*seriously*) Aye, he might make her up some herbal mixture for our Arthur. That might do the trick.

LUCY. He can make a bottle up for you while he's at it. Only my fun—carry on.

LESLIE (*with something on his mind*) Your Fred's not a qualified man.

LIZ. He's an S.R.N.

EZRA. What's an S.R.N.?

LIZ. A State Registered Nurse, and he's a member of the Osteopaths. What more do you want? (*She watches Leslie*)

LESLIE. That's not the same thing, it doesn't make him qualified in a medical sense. See what I mean? I mean, the M.D. You know proper medical qualifications like.

LIZ (*with the air of having found something out*) Go on—keep talkin'. (*She puts down her glass*)

Leslie. Nay, I've done.

Liz. Good—because I haven't started.

Leslie. What do you mean?

(Lucy *rises and puts the glass cloth on the sideboard*)

Liz. I'll tell you what I mean. You wouldn't care if our Violet was a virgin till she was ninety.

(Lucy *turns to listen*)

Leslie. Who? Me? (*He puts down his glass*)

Liz. Yes, you. You've never wanted her to grow up. No, no, it's no use you interrupting, you'll hear me out. She's a grown-up woman and you've treated her like a schoolgirl. You've been thick as thieves —and there's been times when I've felt shut out.

Leslie. If you have it's been your own fault. What about her hair, eh?

Liz. What are you on about now?

(*A sudden thought strikes* Leslie *and he points at Liz*)

Leslie. I'll tell you, the reason you're so upset an' goin' on so much about it is—guilt. Guilt. Yes, guilt.

Liz. Me? Why should I feel guilty?

Leslie (*rising*) Because you egged our Violet into an early marriage.

Liz (*rising*) I only wanted to see the girl happy.

Leslie (*shouting*) You wanted to get her away from the home.

Liz. Why should I?

Leslie. You thought that I'd be that lonely that I couldn't help but turn to you. But it hasn't quite worked out like that, has it?

Liz (*very near to tears*) Don't go too far, Leslie.

(Leslie *turns away up* L. Lucy *moves to* Liz *and sits her* R *of the table*)

Lucy. Try not to say anything you'll be sorry for, Mr Piper. (*She sits above the table*)

Ezra (*after a pause*) What about her 'air? (*He rises and stands with his back to the fire, his glass in his hand*)

Leslie (*crossing to Ezra*) When our Violet was at school she used to have two lovely long plaits. Folk used to turn round in the street an' I hear them saying how lovely they were.

Liz. They were drawing away all her strength. The school doctor said so. (*She makes grunts of interruption during the following*)

Leslie (*ignoring the interruption*) Most nights I used to do her plaits before she went to bed. You always made a hell of a din clattering the pots about in the back kitchen.

Liz. I thought she was getting a bit too drawn towards you. It's not healthy for a girl of that age to get too drawn to her father.

Leslie (*turning to Lucy*) It's coming to something when a girl can't love her own dad.

Lucy. Aye, love's come under suspicion these days. But I see what you mean, Mrs Piper. You don't want them too attached.

Liz (*distressed*) That's it.

(Leslie *turns away up* R)

Ezra (*after a long pause*) Wot about 'er 'air?

Leslie (*turning to Ezra*) I got home from my work one Friday night and when I sat down to my tea, I heard some whispering going on and then our Violet came in. Do you know, for a minute I hardly knew her. Her hair was short and frizzy. She's had it cut and permed or something. I couldn't speak. She rushed across to me and she burst out crying. "I'm sorry, Dad, I'm sorry, Dad," she kept saying. "It's so ugly, I hate it." "Don't blame her," you said, "I persuaded her." You'd gone out of your way just to spite me. I will admit you hurt me. But I haven't bothered you much since, have I?

(Liz *has her head bowed and dabs her eyes with her handkerchief*)

Liz (*after a pause*) I'm sorry, Dad. I were jealous.

Leslie. Nay, lass, don't take on—I understand—now you've come out with it.

(*Voices are heard off in the street.*
Geoffrey, Violet *and* Arthur *enter from the street*)

Violet. Oh! Mum! Dad! (*She crosses to Liz*)

(Liz *tries to cover her distress*)

Geoffrey. Hello—hello, hello! What a surprise.

Arthur (*after a pause*) Oh, hello. Nothing wrong, is there?

(*They all look at him*)

Lucy. That's what we're tryin' to find out, love.

The lights Black-Out *as*—

the Curtain *falls*

Scene 2

Scene—*Fred's garden. The following morning.*
    The house is at an angle L. *From the upstage end of the house, a length of fence runs* R, *broken by a gate. Inside the fence,* R *of the gate, there is a bench, and* L *of the gate there is a rabbit hutch. The house shows one window with a window-box, in which there are three potted geraniums.*

When the Curtain *rises, the stage is empty.* Fred, *wearing his white hospital coat, enters down* L. *He carries a tin bowl with lettuce leaves and clover.*

Fred (*calling over his shoulder*) Come on, Violet, let's have a breath of air, while I feed old Flossie here, m'prize rabbit. (*He feeds the rabbit*) You are hungry, old girl.

(VIOLET *enters down* L, *carrying a large new white photograph album in front of her*)

VIOLET. You've made it nice out here, Uncle Fred. What a lovely lot of flowers you've got. (*She sits on the bench*)

FRED. D'you think so? They've a job to survive in this atmosphere

VIOLET. I expect only the tough 'uns get through.

FRED (*putting down the bowl*) Aye, you could say that. (*He sits* L *of Violet on the bench*) I like to come and sit here after I've been rubbing backs all morning.

VIOLET (*looking up*) It's turned out nice.

FRED. Yes. (*He looks up*) I've a feeling the sun's trying to break through.

(VIOLET *opens the album and looks at the photographs*)

It seems once folk turn fifty in this part of the world, pains set about 'em from every end of the body. (*He looks at the photographs*) I like the full wedding group there.

VIOLET. It's a good one of Geoffrey and me, but I don't think Arthur's come out well on it.

FRED. Happen he's not photogenic. (*He glances at Violet*) 'Course you didn't come all the way out here of a Saturday morning just to show me those wedding pictures.

VIOLET. Geoffrey gave me a lift on his motor bike.

FRED. That wasn't your only reason—I could see you were all tense. Now what's up, love? Get it off your mind.

VIOLET. My mother said I should come and see you.

FRED. What about?

VIOLET. It's about our marriage, Uncle Fred.

FRED. Nothing wrong, is there?

VIOLET. I don't know how to tell you.

FRED. Has Arthur been knocking you about?

VIOLET (*laughing*) Ee, no, nothing like that—I almost wish he had.

FRED (*after a pause*) Oh—what is it, love?

VIOLET (*trying to hold back her emotions*) Uncle Fred. Isn't it awful —I'm—I'm still—I'm still a virgin. (*She bursts into sobs and buries her head on Fred's shoulder*)

(FRED *gently pats Violet, in no hurry to stop her*)

FRED. All right, love, all right. What's so awful about it—why, many a woman would give a fortune to be able to say that.

VIOLET. Not after she'd been a wife for six weeks.

FRED. I see what you mean.

VIOLET. What can be the reason, Uncle Fred?

FRED. We know the reason. You mean what's the cause, what lies behind it. Could be a dozen things.

VIOLET (*after a pause*) Uncle—do you think Arthur might be one of those men who can't find happiness with a woman?

FRED. There are a hell of a lot of men can't find happiness with women—or without 'em, either—but if you mean what I think you mean—the answer is no. What put the blooming idea in your head?

VIOLET. You think of everything when you're lying awake every night. What can it be, then?

FRED. It could be worry—about his job, or trying to get a home together. It could be his surroundings.

VIOLET. But other couples manage all right.

FRED. All couples aren't alike. In fact no two are alike. And you wouldn't think it but even a rabbit can be put off its stroke.

VIOLET. A rabbit!

FRED. Aye, see Flossie here. When she was first ready for mating, the lad from next door brought a lovely big buck called Tom along. There's a special time with animals, see—we needn't go into that. So I opened the door here and we put Tom in. He's scarcely got his nose inside when Flossie set about him—talk about skin an' hair flying.

VIOLET. Did she not fancy him? I love Arthur, y'know.

FRED. Hold on a minute. We kept putting Tom in and taking him out. Even he was getting the wind up.

VIOLET. What happened?

FRED. One day old grandad next door saw us. "Eee, that won't never work," he says. "You can't take the buck to the doe, you'll hatta take the doe to the buck. She's shy in her own place." So's then we took Flossie across to Tom.

VIOLET. What happened?

FRED. That lad's made a fortune. Her's just expecting her sixth litter, aren't you, Flossie?

VIOLET. Oh, but I am in Arthur's home already.

FRED. Nay, you're in his dad's home. Arthur can't walk about with his braces dangling, as they say, an' it's so small, mum an' dad in the next bedroom, Geoff on t'other side.

VIOLET. Oh, Geoff said he'd call for me at twelve.

FRED. What're you always going about with Geoff for?

VIOLET. Well, we're such good pals; we get on like a house on fire.

FRED. Hy, are you sure you've married the right brother?

VIOLET. Eh? Oh, positive. Getting on with somebody is one thing —love is another. Don't you understand that, Uncle Fred? Why, I'll love Arthur to my dying day.

FRED. I see. Violet, are you sure this hitch is all Arthur's fault? Love isn't a one-sided business.

VIOLET. What? But it must be his fault, mustn't it? After all, I'm only a woman.

FRED. *Only!* Speaking as a bachelor, I'd say the woman was most important.

VIOLET. I've never gone against him.

FRED. Against . . . ?

VIOLET. I mean I've always been willing.

FRED. Willing? You need to be more than willing, you need . . .

(*The sound of a motor-cycle horn is heard off* R)

VIOLET. There's Geoffrey now. (*She rises*)

FRED (*rising*) Blimey, girl, next time you must be determined.

(GEOFFREY *enters* R)

GEOFFREY (*moving* C, *above the fence*) Come on, Violet. How go there, Mr Stansfield. Y'know what the traffic's like on Saturday, gal. (*To Fred*) I'm takin' her dancing tonight.

(VIOLET *goes through the gate*)

FRED. Good lad, you.

(GEOFFREY *takes Violet's arm*)

VIOLET (*turning back to Fred*) Do you think it might work out right, Uncle Fred?

FRED. Positive. You love each other, see, an' true love always triumphs. Talk is useless—let love find its own way. God bless. (*He kisses Violet*)

(VIOLET *and* GEOFFREY *exit happily* R. *The sound of the motor-cycle starting up and driving away is heard*)

(*He cups his hands round his mouth and shouts as loud as he can after Violet*) Determined. (*He turns to the rabbit*) Eh, Flossie?

The lights BLACK-OUT *as—*

the CURTAIN *falls*

SCENE 3

SCENE—*A piece of waste ground. A few hours later.*
    The rear entrance and side wall of the cinema where Arthur works is at an angle R. *A stone wall runs from the upstage side of the cinema to* L.

When the CURTAIN *rises,* EDDIE *and* ARTHUR *enter from the cinema, playing with a ball and laughing.*

EDDIE (*crossing to* C) Let's have a game of throwers.

ARTHUR. I'll have a game of anything you want.

EDDIE. Here, I'll bet you don't stop this one.

ARTHUR (*moving* RC) Come on, Jimmy Greaves, let's see.

(JOE *enters from the cinema, stands in the doorway and lights a cigarette. He is dressed up and self-important. He watches the others for a moment or two*)

JOE. Hy, you two!

EDDIE. What's up?

ARTHUR. Hello, there.

JOE. How long are you going to idle it out here?
EDDIE. We're just finishing our teatime.
ARTHUR. Aye, loosening up a bit.
JOE. You don't want all flamin' day for your tea. What do you
think I'm paying you for? Come on, Fitton.
ARTHUR. Sorry—didn't realize our time was up.
JOE (*moving* RC) Well, you realize it now. Get back in your box.
You, too. Playing about with a ball. You're loose enough.
ARTHUR (*moving* R) I was just coming on form.
JOE. You'll never come on form.
ARTHUR. What do you mean—never come on form?
JOE. Nothing. Back in your box an' keep your mind on your work.

(ARTHUR *moves towards the door* R)

EDDIE (*looking at his watch*) By rights, Mr Thompson, our tea half-
hour isn't up yet.

(ARTHUR *stops*)

JOE (*to Eddie*) Don't you be so cheeky.
ARTHUR (*crossing to Eddie*) Are you sure, Eddie?
EDDIE. I'm certain. Positive. We broke at five. Now it's five an'
twenty past. We've another five minutes by rights.

(ARTHUR *grabs the ball and starts playing*)

JOE. What the hell's come over you, Fitton?
ARTHUR. Nothing. I'm just finishing my tea half-hour. Come on,
Eddie. (*He throws the ball to Eddie*)
JOE. You are hell as like!
ARTHUR. You try to stop me.
JOE. You're getting back in there.
ARTHUR. Aye, when I've had my full half hour.

(JOE *is frustrated. He makes a hand swing at Eddie but misses*)

JOE (*to Eddie*) Get in there.
ARTHUR. Don't, Eddie. Insist on your rights.
EDDIE. Do you think I ought?
ARTHUR. Of course. Come on.
JOE (*to Arthur*) You're a nice bloody one to talk about rights.
ARTHUR. What d'you mean?
JOE. You're getting too big for your shoes, Fitton. D'you want
me to do your job for you?
ARTHUR. D'you think you could?
JOE. Do your job—I'd do it on my head. (*To Eddie*) You get in
when I tell you.
EDDIE (*looking at his watch*) We've still got another four minutes.
JOE (*to Arthur*) Yes, on my bloody head. (*He turns to go*)
ARTHUR. I very much doubt it.
JOE (*stopping and turning*) Oh, do you? Come to think of it, I
could do another little job for you, as well. (*To Eddie*) You get
back in there,

(Eddie *crosses to the door* R)

Arthur. What do you mean—what job? (*He senses something and goes tense*)

Joe. Never mind what job—just send for me next time.

Arthur. Send for you? For what? Eh?

Joe. To do a job for that little wife of yours Violet—one it seems you haven't got around to doing. (*To Eddie*) Get back in there. (*To Arthur*) You talking about your rights—what about her bloody rights, eh? (*He gufflaws*) Her conjugal rights. (*He cackles*)

Arthur. You dirty, filthy swine! (*He swings Joe round and hits him in the stomach*)

Joe (*a rough fighter*) Oh ho, if that's how you want it you can have it. Come on, I'll show you a trick or two. (*With expert skill he grabs Arthur by the lapels and swings him round, getting ready to tup him in the face*)

Eddie (*calling*) Look out, Arthur, look out—he's going to tup you with his head. Look out!

(Joe *makes an upward tup with his head to strike Arthur in the face.* Arthur, *in fury, swings his right arm round and takes Joe's arm in an armlock. He pulls Joe's head against his hip and puts on pressure.* Joe *lets out a scream of pain.* Eddie *dances round and applauds.* Arthur *shakes Joe's head*)

Arthur. I'll give you a bloody tuppin'! Say you're sorry. (*He shakes Joe*)

(Joe *howls.*
Molly *enters* L *and crosses to* C. *She is dressed in outdoor clothes for the evening and carries her handbag*)

Joe (*yelling with pain*) You're choking me!

Molly. Hy, hy, what's up? Arthur—is that my . . . ? Hy, let go of him. Can you hear me? Let go. You'll choke him. Let go. Let go when I tell you. Have you gone mad? (*To Eddie*) Help me.

(Arthur *is unheeding.* Molly *slaps him on the back with her handbag, whilst* Arthur, *breathless, seems unaware of her*)

Arthur. Say you're sorry—say you're sorry for bringing my wife's name up.

Eddie. Give it to him, Arthur.

Joe (*finally*) Sorry. (*Choking*) I'm sorry, blast you!

(Arthur, *with a last jerk, sends* Joe *flying.* Joe *nurses his throat.* Molly *has heard Arthur's words about his wife and a perceptible change comes over her, but she keeps up her show*)

Molly. Get off, you nearly choked him. (*To Joe*) Are you all right, Joe?

Arthur (*very loud and angry*) I wish I had.

Molly. I never thought you had it in you. What's it all about? What happened?

JOE (*to Molly*) Get the hell out of it.

EDDIE. Good lad you, Arthur, that'll stop him bringing your wife up.

JOE. Get in. You get in there.

MOLLY (*to Eddie*) What's happened? Tell me what happened.

EDDIE (*surprised; innocently*) He said something about Arthur and his wife——

JOE (*interrupting*) You get back to your work.

EDDIE. —Something about doing a job for him.

(MOLLY *turns on* JOE)

Send for me next time, he said. It upset Arthur.

MOLLY (*turning to Arthur*) Ee, I'm right sorry, love. That he'd say anything about you and that lovely little girl you married.

JOE (*angrily*) Fitton, you're sacked—that's your lot.

ARTHUR. Go and stick your bloody job!

(ARTHUR *exits* R. EDDIE *now watches with some anticipation as* MOLLY *turns to* JOE)

JOE (*turning on Eddie; roaring*) Get in there when you're told.

EDDIE (*calmly looking at his watch*) I've another minute and a half left yet.

MOLLY (*quietly holding it all under*) You promised you would never breathe a word—but the first one you tell is the poor lad himself. I could die of shame.

JOE. He drew it out of me.

MOLLY. Drew it out of you—I wish he'd choked the daylights out of you—to say a thing like that. (*She pauses*) You do a job for him—you—you flamin' old two in one, why you couldn't do a job for our cat—you're all talk—all bloody talk. I've a good min' to . . . (*She sets about Joe with her handbag*) You do a job! You wouldn't know where to start—you—why, the flaming laundryman has been doing a job for you for years. An' doing it better than you'd know how.

JOE *yells out as* MOLLY *lambasts him and* EDDIE *cheers.*
JOE *exits to the cinema.*
MOLLY, *still beating* JOE, *follows him off.*
EDDIE, *thumping the ball with his hands, follows them off, and the lights* BLACK-OUT *as—*

the CURTAIN *falls*

SCENE 4

SCENE—*The Fittons' home. That evening.*

When the CURTAIN *rises, the living-room is lit and the bedroom is in darkness.* EZRA *is seated* L *of the table, starting his tea, a plate of bubble and squeak. He is in his shirt-sleeves and has his Saturday evening suit on. He wears his glasses. A copy of the "Bolton Evening News" is propped up in front of him. He shakes large quantities of sauce over his food, then mixes it with his knife and turns it over. He takes a long time doing this. LUCY enters from the kitchen, carrying a pot of tea. She stands above the table, puts down the teapot and pours milk into a mug.*

LUCY. You look as though you're mixing concrete.

EZRA. Do you mind mindin' your own business? (*He continues to mix*)

(LUCY *sighs and watches him.* EZRA *starts eating, but stops chewing when he tastes the first mouthful*)

LUCY (*pouring tea for Ezra*) I thought you'd put too much on. (*She sits above the table*)

EZRA. There isn't enough. (*He adds more sauce to his meal*)

(ARTHUR *enters suddenly from the street and crosses towards the door up* R)

LUCY (*without looking up*) Ee, hello, Geoff. (*She suddenly realizes it is not Geoffrey and looks up in surprise*) Oh. Is it you? I thought it was our Geoff. What's brought you home at this hour? (*She sees Arthur's stormy face*) Nothing wrong, is there? (*She rises and moves* R)

ARTHUR (*very upset*) No, Mother, it's all right.

EZRA. Have you got the sack?

(ARTHUR *looks at Ezra, decides to say nothing and exits up* R *to the stairs*)

Now what's up with him?

LUCY. He looked upset. (*She moves above the table*)

EZRA. Did he say why he'd come home at this hour?

LUCY. You were here.

EZRA. Why didn't you ask him?

LUCY (*pouring a cup of tea*) Why didn't you?

EZRA. I won't have him walking through the house like it was a public convenience.

LUCY. Don't be vulgar! Something's upset him. I'll go and take him a cup of tea.

EZRA. Go on, go and mard him. (*He taps his mug for more tea*)

(VIOLET *enters from the street*)

LUCY. Ee, hello, love.

EZRA. Hello, Violet.

VIOLET. Hello. Is Geoffrey back yet?

EZRA. Not yet—why?

VIOLET. Good. (*She removes her coat and hangs it on the pegs* L) He's takin' me dancing. (*She crosses up* R)

LUCY. Our Arthur's just come home.

VIOLET (*stopping and turning; surprised*) He has! Why? Nothin' wrong, is there?

LUCY. He didn't say.

EZRA. He walked through here like it were a public convenience.

LUCY. Don't talk like that at table. (*She hands the cup of tea to Violet*) He seemed a bit quiet, love. Will you take him his cup of tea up?

VIOLET. I hope there's nothin' wrong. (*She senses something and feels guilty*)

LUCY. Here, and this piece of cake. (*She puts a piece of cake on the saucer*)

(VIOLET *exits up* R *to the stairs*)

Something's upset our Arthur.

(*The lights fade in the living-room and come up in the bedroom, where* ARTHUR *is packing his canvas grip. He is doing it in a determined and methodical way, picking up one or two books and putting them in. There is a mixture of regret and determination to leave. The grip is on the ottoman down* C.

VIOLET *enters, carrying the cup of tea*)

VIOLET. I've brought you a cup of tea, Arthur.

(ARTHUR *crosses to the bookshelves* R, *gets two more books and returns to the ottoman*)

Arthur!

(ARTHUR *ignores Violet and puts the books in the grip*)

Arthur—what's the matter? (*She pauses*)

(ARTHUR *collects a shirt from the bed*)

Arthur, I'm speaking to you.

ARTHUR (*putting the shirt in the grip*) I heard you.

VIOLET. Then why don't you answer me?

ARTHUR (*moving to the bed and collecting his pyjamas*) I've nothin' to say.

(VIOLET *stands, silent and shocked, with the tea in her hand.* ARTHUR *moves to the grip*)

VIOLET (*crossing to* R *of him*) What are you doing?

ARTHUR (*stuffing the pyjamas into the grip*) Packing.

VIOLET. Why—where are you going?

ARTHUR (*moving to the dressing-table*) Getting out.

VIOLET. You're what?

ARTHUR. I'm leaving you. (*He takes a shirt from the dressing-table drawer*)

VIOLET. No! Why—what have I done?

ARTHUR (*putting the shirt in the grip*) You've opened your big mouth once too often.

VIOLET. Arthur! What are you saying?

ARTHUR (*moving to* L *of her*) I asked you not to tell anybody. I begged you.

VIOLET. But I haven't—I only told my mother.

ARTHUR. And your father!

VIOLET. What . . . ? Yes.

ARTHUR. That's what you were all three yapping about yesterday, wasn't it?

VIOLET. My dad came in . . .

(ARTHUR *moves around picking things up and packing them*)

ARTHUR (*with bitterness and anger*) What did you go to your Uncle Fred's for today?

VIOLET. My mother said I should.

ARTHUR. What? To talk me over with the family quack?

VIOLET. What's happened, Arthur?

ARTHUR (*bitterly and quietly*) I'm nobody an' nothing—an' I don't mind—for at least I've always been able to hold my head up in the neighbourhood. Then I'm no sooner married—I'll admit I made a poor show of it—than my own wife goes around discussing our private life with everybody. An' now I'm a bloody laughing-stock. Do you realize I can never face these people again?

VIOLET. But listen, Arthur—I haven't . . .

ARTHUR (*shouting*) You haven't, then how the hell can dirty Joe tell me he'll come round and do a job for me with my wife—one I can't manage, eh?

VIOLET (*very upset for Arthur*) Oh, Arthur, I'm so sorry—but I didn't tell anybody . . .

ARTHUR. Liar! Bloody liar! (*He grabs her, shakes her, and sends the cup of tea flying*) I could . . . (*He changes his mind and shoves her away, then turns back to his packing. With a sudden bitter thought, said to hurt Violet*) I hope you told him that you always put me off—yes, from the first night you couldn't stop laughing. You put me off.

(VIOLET *is shocked and humiliated, but a touch of pluck saves her. She gives Arthur a hard slap across the face*)

(*Furiously*) Why—you—you bloody little bitch—I'll—I'll . . .

VIOLET. You'll what?

ARTHUR. I'll—I'll . . .

(VIOLET *pushes* ARTHUR. *He grabs her. Together they fall on the bed and struggle for a moment, then they begin to kiss passionately, their bodies coming close together as the lights fade in the bedroom and come up in the living-room where* EZRA *and* LUCY *are still at the table.* EZRA *has finished his bubble and squeak, is eating bread and jam and drinking his tea. His glasses are still on his nose and is reading his paper.* LUCY *is eating bread and butter*)

EZRA (*glancing upwards*) Did you hear that, Lucy?

LUCY. I heard nothing. (*She continues to eat*)

EZRA. I coulda swore I heard a noise. . .

LUCY. You're hearing things.

EZRA (*referring to his newspaper*) Know what it says here—if the Chinese carry on increasin', there's not going to be enough food to go round in fifty years' time.

LUCY. You should worry about that.

EZRA. Who's to tell these Chinese not to carry on like that?

LUCY. I doubt they'd take any notice if you told 'em. (*She refills Ezra's mug*)

(*They continue to eat throughout*)

EZRA. It's funny our Arthur and Violet haven't come down by this. I wonder what's keeping 'em.

LUCY. You keep on troublin' yourself about the Chinese—you'll have enough on your plate.

(GEOFFREY *enters from the street, carrying a large, light parcel which he puts on the piano stool* L)

GEOFFREY (*his usual breezy self*) Hello! Hello! Hello! Is me tea ready, Mum?

LUCY (*rising*) It's in the oven. I'll get it.

(LUCY *exits to the kitchen*)

GEOFFREY (*removing his raincoat and scarf*) Has Violet come back yet then, Dad? (*He hangs his raincoat and scarf on the pegs* L)

EZRA. Her's upstairs.

GEOFFREY. Upstairs?

EZRA. Aye. Upstairs.

(GEOFFREY *moves up* R.
     LUCY *enters from the kitchen with a plate of food*)

LUCY (*intercepting Geoffrey*) Where are you going?

GEOFFREY. Upstairs. I'll call Violet. I'm taking her to the *Palais*.

LUCY. Don't. (*She puts the plate at the place set* R *of the table*)

GEOFFREY. Don't what?

LUCY. Don't disturb her.

GEOFFREY (*bewildered*) Disturb her? I'm not disturbing her. (*He moves to* R *of the table*) I'm taking her dancing.

LUCY. Her husband's with her. (*She sits above the table*)

GEOFFREY. Her what's with her?

LUCY. Her husband, you mug! Our Arthur.

GEOFFREY (*contemptuously*) Oh, him! (*He takes two tickets from his pocket and puts them on the table beside his plate*) What's he doin' home at this hour? (*He removes his jacket, hangs it on the back of the chair* R *of the table, sits* R *of the table and commences his meal*)

LUCY. He's minding his own business.

EZRA. He walked through here like it were a public convenience.

LUCY (*rising*) If you mention that thing again I won't be responsible. (*She pours a cup of tea for Geoffrey*)

EZRA. There's no other way of puttin' it. He looked neither left nor right.

LUCY. I warned you—now shut up! (*She lifts the teapot threateningly*)

GEOFFREY. Why are you getting so ratty over a public convenience, Mum?

Lucy. Because when I was a girl I once went walkin' into a men's place by mistake. I saw this line of men with stooped backs an' their bloomin' heads sunk forward. They were all wearing raincoats and looked as though they were expecting to be shot in the back at any minute. The sight of it has never left my mind. (*She pauses and sits above the table*) If ever I have a nightmare you can bet that comes into it.

Geoffrey (*after a pause*) Dad, d'you think our Arthur's got the sack or somethin'?

Ezra. I don't know what he's got. It's no business of mine, but he had no right to walk through here . . .

(Lucy *rises threateningly, teapot in hand*)

Well, he did!

Geoffrey (*rising and turning to go up* r) I think I'll . . .

Lucy (*catching Geoffrey's sleeve*) You'll sit down an' have your tea —you have me on the go from mornin' till night. (*She resumes her seat*)

Geoffrey (*sitting* r *of the table*) Right, Mum. (*He pauses*) But suppose I give a shout up so she'll know I'm here—just to be on the safe side.

Lucy. You will not. She doesn't want to know you're here. Eat your tea.

Geoffrey. How do you know she doesn't want to know I'm here?

Lucy (*after a slight pause*) I've got a feelin'. Ever had one? Besides, she's with her husband.

Ezra. It's no use tryin' to get the better of your mother, lad— she'll have the last word.

Lucy. What've you got in the parcel?

Geoffrey. Oh—a pair of love-birds.

Ezra. Come off it.

Geoffrey. Like to see 'um? (*He rises, crosses to the parcel and removes the wrapping, revealing a bird-cage with a pair of small brilliant love-birds*)

(*The birds start to sing.* Ezra *rises and crosses to* l. Lucy *rises and joins the other two around the cage.* Ezra *and* Lucy *are intensely interested*)

Ezra (*charmed*) Ee, are they for us?

Geoffrey. For you? Are they hell as like!

Lucy. Aah, how bonny! What lovely colours. Ee, harken 'um.

Ezra. Is them 'um singing?

Geoffrey. You don't think it's me, do you?

Ezra. What do they do?

Lucy. What do you think? They're love-birds.

Ezra. They're quite quaint, aren't they?

Geoffrey. They're a weddin' present, like. Shall I take 'em up an' show Violet? (*He picks up the cage*)

Lucy (*moving above the table*) No, she'll be comin' down. (*She makes a space on the table for the cage*)

(GEOFFREY *puts the cage on the downstage side of the table*)

EZRA. Did you get 'um cheap? (*He sits L of the table*)

(LUCY *sits above the table*)

GEOFFREY. Not cheap but handy. I got the cage thrown in an'
I couldn't resist the bargain. (*He puts the wrapping on the stool down R,
then sits R of the table*)

EZRA. Will they breed?

GEOFFREY. I'm not sure.

LUCY. I don't think so. Not in captivity. (*She eats her bread and
butter*)

(*The birds stop singing*)

EZRA. Puts 'em off like. Fancy that. (*He peers into the cage*)

LUCY. Keep your big face away from the cage—you'll frighten
'um. Ee, watch 'um kiss!

EZRA. Ee, I thought they were peckin' one another.

LUCY. You would.

GEOFFREY. Y'know what the chap said, he said they'd die if they
were separated.

EZRA. Get off!

GEOFFREY. Aye, they pine away like.

EZRA. Fancy, they don't weigh an ounce between the pair of
'um, an' they've more feeling than a Christian.

(*There is a knock at the street door*)

LUCY. Sumdy at door.

EZRA (*rising and picking up his paper and mug of tea*) Cover 'um up
quick, Geoff.

GEOFFREY (*rising*) Why, what's up?

(LUCY *rises and goes to the street door*)

EZRA (*crossing to the fireplace*) It doesn't look nice of a Sat'day
evening. Love-birds on the table. You never know what folk think.
Might give a wrong impression, see.

(GEOFFREY *looks at Ezra in surprise, picks up the cage, puts it on the
stool down R and covers it with the wrapping.* LUCY *opens the door*)

LUCY. Ee, come in, Mrs Piper. How are you?

(LIZ *enters from the street*)

EZRA. Good evenin', Mrs Piper. (*He sits in the armchair*)

LIZ (*moving up L of the table*) Now don't let me disturb you. Hello,
Mr Fitton. Geoff, love, get on with your tea. I'll tell you what it is,
Leslie just got home with the news that there's a little house for sale
might suit our Violet and Arthur.

(GEOFFREY *sits R of the table*)

EZRA. They've got no money, have they?

LUCY. Don't be so quick.

GEOFFREY. Well, they haven't. An' our Arthur won't go in debt.

LUCY. Hush a minute. Where is it, Mrs Piper?

LIZ. Near Belhill reservoir, y' know, up Bellhill brew.

GEOFFREY. Oh, ay, that little row of stone cottages. Them's nice, they are.

LIZ. He'll let it go for seven hundred pounds.

LUCY. That sounds like a bargain.

EZRA. You coulda bought 'um for fifty quid apiece one time of day.

LUCY. Go on, Mrs Piper.

LIZ (*sitting* L *of the table*) It needs a bit doin' to it. But Leslie reckons it'll come up lovely after beautifying.

LUCY (*moving above the table; gently*) Would you have a look at it, Dad? Cup of tea, Mrs Piper?

EZRA. What's the use? Our Arthur will take no notice of me.

LIZ. I wouldn't say no if there's one going, Mrs Fitton.

(LUCY *gets a cup and saucer from the sideboard cupboard, puts them on the table and pours a cup of tea for Liz*)

Where's our Violet got to?

GEOFFREY (*eagerly*) She's upstairs. (*He rises*) I'll give her a shout. Tell her you're here. (*He seems eager to break it up*)

LUCY (*pushing Geoffrey back on his chair*) You'll stay where you are. Leave Violet a-be.

GEOFFREY. What's come over you, Mum?

LIZ (*puzzled*) Eh? Why? Is there anythin' up?

(GEOFFREY *cannot make out what is up but has an unconscious desire to interrupt whatever might be going on upstairs.* EZRA *is sublimely ignorant of everything except how Arthur walked through the room.* LIZ *has no idea what is going on.* LUCY *has a deep intuition about these matters*)

LUCY (*with meaning*) Our Arthur's upstairs with her. (*She puts the cup of tea in front of Liz then clears Geoffrey's plate to the sideboard*)

LIZ (*missing the point*) Your Arthur! (*She pauses*) What's he doin' at home at this hour?

EZRA. He never said. He walked through here like it were a pub . . .

(LUCY *turns, grabs the teapot and threatens Ezra with it.* EZRA *subsides into his paper*)

GEOFFREY (*fed up*) I'm supposed to be takin' Violet to a dance· I've got the tickets. Paid for 'um.

LIZ. Ee, have you, really? (*She looks upwards. After a pause*) It'll be a pity if they miss the house—and the dance. (*She still has not cottoned on. She looks at Geoffrey*)

GEOFFREY (*hopefully*) I could just give a call, Mum.

LUCY (*sitting above the table*) I said "no". You're like all single folk, not a jot of respect for married privacy. Once you get married you want folk to come barging into your bedroom any hours of the day and night. (*She turns and gives a very significant look to Liz with a nod of the head*)

(Liz *is puzzled for a moment. She turns away and faces the audience, her face somewhat bewildered. Then slowly the significance of it dawns on her and she turns to Lucy and gives her a look.* Lucy *nods.* Ezra *is now reading his newspaper and has no idea of this*)

Liz (*desperately making conversation*) The weather can't make up its mind, can it?

Ezra (*over his paper*) Y'what?

Liz. I say the weather—it can't make up its mind.

Ezra (*after a pause*) I thought it looked like rain once over.

Liz. Yes, when the wind dropped, about five o'clock. I said to Leslie, we're going to have some rain.

Ezra. It came over quite dark and low-lying one time.

Liz. Yes, an' the next thing it all seemed to blow over just as if nothing were.

(Geoffrey, *who does not quite know why he is so eager to shout upstairs, keeps staring at Ezra and Liz as they go on talking, turning his head from one side to the other*)

Ezra. I thought I felt a spot or two.

Liz. Ee, I never knew it had sent any down.

Ezra. That was my impression, that I got one or two on the back of my head. Not that I'd swear on it that it was rain.

Lucy (*rising*) Excuse me.

(Lucy *exits to the kitchen*)

Liz. You can never be sure when you only get a few drops of wet what they are or where they're from. I've often felt 'um when nobody else has.

Ezra (*sagely*) The odd drop can come from anywhere. But when you get a few drops followin' you about, you can almost swear it's rain.

Geoffrey (*unexpectedly*) Naturally if it's followin' you about.

Ezra. Y'what?

Geoffrey. I say—if wet follows you about it's bound to be rain.

Ezra. You're too late, lad. That's the conclusion I just reached with Mrs Piper? Eh, Mrs Piper?

Liz. Yes, Mr Fitton.

(*There is a knock at the street door*)

Ezra. Somebody at door, Geoff.

Geoffrey (*rising*) I'm not deaf. (*He crosses to the street door and opens it*) Hello, Mr Piper.

(Leslie *enters by the street door*)

Leslie. Hello, Geoff. How go there! (*To Liz*) Have you told her?

Liz. Told who what?

LESLIE. Who d'you think—our Violet about the house.

LIZ. She's upstairs.

LESLIE. Upstairs? What's she doing upstairs? Can't you call her?

GEOFFREY (*crossing to the door up* R) I will, Mr Piper.

(LUCY *enters from the kitchen*)

LUCY (*to Geoffrey*) Where are you off?

GEOFFREY. I'm just calling Violet.

LUCY. You're doing nothing of the sort.

GEOFFREY. What's up with you, Mum? Mr Piper wants to see Violet.

LUCY. Happen Violet doesn't want to see Mr Piper. Sit down, Mr Piper.

LESLIE (*sitting above the table*) If she doesn't want to see me, Mrs Fitton, it'll be for the first time in her life.

LUCY. There's has to be a first time for everything.

LIZ. Just what I was thinking.

EZRA (*to Leslie*) Has it blown over?

LESLIE. Has what blown over?

GEOFFREY. Oh, blimey, not again!

LUCY. What's come over you?

EZRA. He's hoppin' about like a cat on hot bricks.

LESLIE (*rising*) Well, I'll be off.

LIZ. What're you going off for?

LESLIE. I thought I'd slip round to the cinema and tell Arthur about the house.

LIZ. He's not there.

LESLIE. Where is he?

EZRA. He's upstairs with your Violet.

LESLIE. What's he doing at home at this hour?

EZRA. He didn't say—he walked through here like it were . . .

(LUCY *lets out a groan and turns on Ezra as though about to murder him.* LESLIE *looks on this with alarm. Footsteps and a door slamming are heard off upstairs.* LIZ *rises and moves* L)

GEOFFREY (*moving down* R) They're coming down.

(*They all look towards the door up* R. EZRA *rises and moves to the fireplace.*

VIOLET *and* ARTHUR *enter up* R *from the stairs.* VIOLET *is looking radiant. She carries a travelling coat and her handbag.* ARTHUR *is looking confident. He carries a suitcase. Both look happy*)

I thought you were never comin' down.

VIOLET. Ee, hello, Mum. Hello, Dad. Nice to see you. (*She crosses and kisses both Liz and Leslie warmly*)

LIZ. Ee, hello, love.

ARTHUR (*putting the case on the floor up* C) Hello, Mrs Piper. Hello there, Mr Piper.

(LUCY *is smiling. She is quick on the uptake.* EZRA *is unsure of himself.* LIZ *is pleased.* GEOFFREY *has had his nose put out of joint*)

LESLIE. Hello, lad.

LIZ. Hullo, Arthur.

LUCY (*to Arthur*) Did you get your cup of tea, love?

ARTHUR (R *of Violet; his arm around her*) Eh? Oh—ta.

GEOFFREY. Hy, what's the suitcase for? Are you goin' some-where?

VIOLET. Yes, we're going on our honeymoon.

GEOFFREY. Where are you goin' then?

ARTHUR. Blackpool—eh, Vi?

VIOLET. Yes. (*She puts her coat and bag on top of the suitcase*)

LIZ. Ee, Arthur, where your mam an' dad went.

EZRA. Just the two of you?

VIOLET. I hope so.

EZRA. Has Joe Thompson given you time off from your job?

ARTHUR. I've got no job.

EZRA. Y'mean you've finished?

ARTHUR. Yip. I squeezed that chap's head a bit. For not mindin' his own business.

LUCY (*jubilantly*) That deserves a new pot of tea.

(LUCY *grabs the teapot and exits eagerly to the kitchen*)

ARTHUR. Anyway, I'll be going into the police force when I get back.

GEOFFREY. You can't! They won't have you—not till you've put that half inch on.

ARTHUR. Know what—I've a feeling I've put it on.

GEOFFREY. Get off! How could you?

ARTHUR. I only said I'd a feeling.

VIOLET. You are taller. (*To the others*) Don't you think so?

LESLIE. Could be—could be.

EZRA. I wonder how that came about?

(LUCY *enters from the kitchen with a pot of tea*)

LUCY. What came about?

EZRA. Our Arthur's just grown half an inch, Lucy.

LUCY (*putting the pot on the table*) What about it?

EZRA. I dunno. I was only telling you.

GEOFFREY. Wut about the dance, Vi? I've got the tickets.

VIOLET. Ee, I couldn't dance for toffee tonight. I don't know why, but my legs feel all funny.

(GEOFFREY *sits on the pouffe down* R. LIZ *crosses, stands between Violet and Arthur and puts her arms around them*)

LIZ. We've got some news for you.

VIOLET. What's that, Mam?

LIZ. Your dad's heard of a house goin'. Up near Bellhill Reservoir. One of them old stone cottages with garden.

ARTHUR. How much a week is it?

LESLIE. He's selling it. Seven hundred pounds.

VIOLET. That's a lot of money.

LESLIE. It's a right bargain.

(LUCY *whispers to* ARTHUR, *but he hesitates and shakes his head.* EZRA *has his back to the others and is filling his pipe at the mantelpiece.* ARTHUR *hesitates.* LUCY *pushes him towards Ezra*)

ARTHUR (*moving to* L *of Ezra*) What do you think, Dad?

EZRA (*turning slowly; astonished*) Eh? Were you speakin' to me, lad?

ARTHUR. About this cottage. I'd like your advice before I did anything. I mean, you'd know better than anybody else.

(*They all look at Ezra*)

EZRA. My advice—what I say is, buy the bloody house.

LUCY (*in support*) That's right, Dad. (*She gets a cup and saucer from the sideboard cupboard, puts them on the table and pours a cup of tea*)

(LIZ *murmurs approvingly*)

EZRA. You can't go far wrong with bricks and mortar. Every young couple should have their own home, where they can feel at ease and happy.

(VIOLET *sits above the table.* LUCY *puts the cup of tea in front of Violet.* ARTHUR *and* EZRA *talk together, apart from the others*)

ARTHUR. It's the money, that's the problem.

EZRA (*gruffly*) Don't let money stand in the way. I've a bob or two. Leave the money side of it to me, lad.

ARTHUR. Thank you very much, Dad, but I couldn't come on you for that.

(LIZ *sits* L *of the table*)

EZRA (*gruffly; almost aggressively*) Why not? You're my son, aren't you? It 'ud be a damn poor father who couldn't help his own lad out. (*He has to shut up because the gruffness is running out*)

ARTHUR. Ta, Dad, ta, very much. It's good to know I've got you behind me.

EZRA. We all need somebody.

GEOFFREY. A pity—you'll hatta cut out your honeymoon now, eh?

LUCY. Nay, you can't do that.

LIZ. No, don't put it off. A honeymoon doesn't stand being put off too often—does it, Mrs Fitton?

LUCY. Not likely. It always something to look back on and remember.

EZRA. I'll look at the cottage for you.

ARTHUR. If you would Dad. I could depend on your judgement.

LUCY (*moving to* L *of Arthur and patting his shoulder*) Well, of course you could.

EZRA. And if there's any plasterin' and what not to be done, our Geoffrey will give me a hand, won't you, Geoff?

GEOFFREY (*still befogged*) What's that?

LUCY. Plasterin'. Hy, their present.

GEOFFREY (*rising*) Oh, aye, I forgot. (*His good nature now comes out. He picks up the cage, removes the wrapping and puts the cage on the table*) Love-birds, Violet, for you an' our Arthur.

VIOLET. Ee, how bonny! Listen to 'em, Arthur.

(*The birds sing*)

ARTHUR. They're nice. Thanks, Geoff.

(EZRA *takes a wad of banknotes from his trousers pocket and flips through them*)

VIOLET. Ta, very much indeed, Geoff.

GEOFFREY. It's all right.

ARTHUR. Would you keep an eye on 'em, Geoff, till we get back?

GEOFFREY. Eh? Oh—sure, sure, I will. (*He picks up the cage and looks rather forlorn to be left with the love-birds. He puts the cage on the table* L)

LIZ. Yes, you'd better be gettin' goin'. (*She rises and moves* L)

LESLIE. Yes, they had.

(VIOLET *rises and moves to* LIZ *to say good-bye.* EZRA *beckons to* ARTHUR, *who moves to* L *of him*)

EZRA (*gruffly*) Are you carryin'? Have you any ready cash? (*He taps his pocket*)

ARTHUR. I've got my Post Office savings book, Dad.

EZRA. Here—just in case. (*He slips Arthur some notes*) Always have money in thy pocket. It's the only way. (*He feels a bit clumsy over giving*)

ARTHUR (*pocketing the notes*) Ta, Dad. I'll see you right. Now, about the cottage . . .

EZRA. Leave it all in my hands.

ARTHUR. Thanks, Dad. That'll set my mind at rest. (*He holds out his hand*) Well, good-bye.

(EZRA *looks at Arthur's outstretched hand and takes it with held down emotion*)

EZRA. Good-bye an' God bless thee, lad. An' never be short whilst I have it.

(ARTHUR *moves to Lucy and kisses her.* VIOLET *moves to Ezra*)

VIOLET. Good-bye, Mr Fitton, and thanks. (*She kisses Ezra*)

EZRA. Look after him, love.

(VIOLET *collects her coat and bag.* ARTHUR *picks up the suitcase. They all make farewells, a very warm parting.* EZRA *stands there staring in front of him like a man in a dream.*

VIOLET *and* ARTHUR *exit to the street. The others wave and call "God-speed", etc., then it goes silent in the room*)

LIZ (*by the door; moved*) Didn't they make a bonny couple?

LESLIE. I've never seen our Violet as pretty.

LUCY (*moving up* C; *with a sob*) Aye, they looked made for each other.

GEOFFREY (*closing the street door*) I thought our Arthur looked quite different, Mum.

EZRA (*sitting* R *of the table*) He's a good lad, is yon.

LIZ. I've always said Arthur was reliable.

(LUCY *tidies the crockery on the table*)

EZRA. Y'know who he put me in mind of, Lucy, the way he went off with that walk? (*He avoids saying his friend's name and slowly droops his head*)

(LUCY *puts a comforting hand on Ezra's shoulder but turns her head away*)

GEOFFREY (*after a pause; in a concerned whisper*) Mum—what's up with Dad? He's crying?

EZRA. I can cry if I want, can't I? (*He wipes his eyes*) It's life, lad, life. It might make you laugh at your age, but one day it'll make you bloody cry.

The love-birds are heard singing as—

the CURTAIN *slowly falls*

ALL IN GOOD TIME

A Comedy

BILL NAUGHTON

Revised Edition

ALL IN GOOD TIME

The play can be performed in one set throughout if the following substitutions are made for Act II, Scenes 2 and 3.

ACT II

SCENE 2

SCENE—*The Fitton home. The following morning.*

As the CURTAIN *rises* VIOLET *is seen combing her wet hair. She is wearing a pretty housecoat, and there is a towel round her shoulders.*

VIOLET (*calls*) Geoffrey! Geoffrey! Could you fetch me my hair dryer, please—I've left it on the kitchen table.

(*A pause, then enter* GEOFFREY *wearing casual motor-bike gear, looking bright and fresh, ready for going out. He is carrying the hair-dryer*)

GEOFFREY. Who peeled your grapes before you met me! Here y'are. (*He puts the dryer on the table*)

VIOLET. Ta very much. And where are you off?

GEOFFREY. Guess what—I'm thinking of going getting you a wedding present.

VIOLET. Getting *me* one!

GEOFFREY. Well, you and your old man.

VIOLET. You've left it a bit late, haven't you! (*She sits R of the table, picks up the dryer and starts to dry her hair*)

GEOFFREY. I've had my eye on something, see, and——

VIOLET (*cuts in*) —And you were waiting for the sales commencing.

GEOFFREY. How did you guess! And then I'm off to collect the tickets for that dance I'm taking you tonight. Make a good job of your hair—I want you to look bonny. Then all my other girls will be dead jealous . . .

VIOLET. I say, Geoff—you couldn't be a darling and run me over to my Uncle Fred's on your way?

GEOFFREY. What do you want to go round to him for—to get your back rubbed! Here, I'll rub it for you.

(GEOFFREY *gives a joking rub to her back, then takes the hair-dryer and starts to dry Violet's hair*)

Nice little back you've got! Whew . . . a smashing vertebrae. . . . Well, I might take you if you hurry up. And after the dance there's going to be a party at Harry's place—a right old rave up that'll be. Shall I take you with me?

VIOLET. Your Arthur might not like it. I mean if I got back late.

GEOFFREY. Our Arthur! . . . He won't mind what time you get in.

VIOLET. No, I don't suppose he will.

GEOFFREY (*pause*) Nothing wrong—is there, Vi?

VIOLET. Geoffrey, do you think I'm attractive—you can tell me frankly—I won't mind—or am I a dead loss—I mean, would I put a man off?

(GEOFFREY *plays it cool and takes a weighing-up look at Violet*)

GEOFFREY. I wouldn't say you were a dead loss—no. And you wouldn't put me off . . . but on the other hand, I think perhaps you need to let yourself go a bit more.

(GEOFFREY *stoops and gives Violet a warm, brotherly kiss. Something prompts* VIOLET *to put on the pressure, and she returns the kiss with a show of sudden and unexpected passion.* GEOFFREY *is at first baffled and for a moment he doesn't know how to take it: then it is almost shattering as he finds* VIOLET *can let herself go.*

There is a knocking on the street door. GEOFFREY *is recovering himself when* VIOLET *breaks away*)

VIOLET. There's somebody at the door.

GEOFFREY (*dazed*) What . . . ? Eh? . . .

(*Further knocking at the door*)

VIOLET. Somebody at the door! . . .

(GEOFFREY *stares in a dazed way at Violet for a moment and then seems almost to stagger across to the door. The effect is slightly comic, even on Violet.* GEOFFREY *pulls himself together, then opens the door*)

GEOFFREY. Hello there! (*Turns*) Vi, it's your uncle—your Uncle Fred. Come in, Fred, will you. How nice to see you. . . .

(*Enter* UNCLE FRED)

VIOLET. Oh, hello, Uncle Fred!

FRED. Hello, love! (*Pause*) Are you two all alone?

(GEOFFREY *and* VIOLET *look uncomfortably at each other for a moment*)

GEOFFREY. Aye, they've all gone off somewhere or other.

VIOLET. And Geoff was just going off, too, when you knocked.

GEOFFREY. Aye, I were! And Violet was about to go up to your place.

FRED (*to Violet*) You were! Whatever for?

VIOLET (*awkward pause*) Oh, nothing. (*Idea*) Oh, I was going to bring our wedding pictures and let you have a look at them.

(GEOFFREY *picks up the album and puts it down in front of Fred*)

GEOFFREY. Aye, here—have a look now. Well, I'll be off. See you tonight, Vi. Don't be late! (*To Fred*) I'm taking her to a dance.

(GEOFFREY *winks and is off. Ad lib. bye-bye, ta-ra, etc., as he exits.*
FRED *is looking at the pictures*)

FRED. He's a nice fresh sort of lad is Geoff.

VIOLET. Yes, isn't he! Shall I make you a cup of tea, Uncle
Fred?

FRED. No thanks, love, I only called in passing. I'll have to be
on my way. Ee, I like this one—the four of you.

VIOLET. Yes, it's a good one of Geoff—and I don't look too bad
—but I don't think Arthur's come out so well on it.

FRED. Ah well, happen he's not photogenic. Where is he, by the
way?

VIOLET. Oh, he went off with Eddie. They always have their
children's matinee Saturday—then they both come back here for
their tea-break.

FRED. Any news about your getting a house yet?

VIOLET. No, not yet. You get as you lose heart.

FRED. Don't do that, love—whatever else you do.

(*They look at each other a bit awkwardly as though* FRED *had un-
knowingly struck a sore spot.* FRED *dismisses the album*)

Yes, they're very nice wedding pictures, love . . . but you weren't
thinking of coming all the way out to me just to show me those,
were you? (*Pause*) Come on, love. What's wrong?

VIOLET. My mother said I should come and see you, Uncle
Fred.

FRED. Oh, she did—and what about?

VIOLET. I don't like telling you.

FRED. Oh, come off it. You know you can tell me anything. . . .

VIOLET. It's about Arthur—about our marriage . . .

FRED. Oh—what about him—has he started knocking you
about already?

VIOLET (*laughs*) Oh, no, nothing like that . . . far from it.

FRED What is it, then?

VIOLET. Uncle Fred—isn't it awful—I'm . . . ooh, I hate saying
it—but I'm still . . . I'm still a virgin.

(VIOLET *can keep up her control no longer and she turns and buries her
face against Fred's shoulder, sobbing.* FRED *pats her gently and lets her
cry*)

FRED. All right, love . . . all right . . . what's so awful about it.
There's many a woman would give a fortune to be able to say that!

VIOLET. Yes . . . but not after she'd been married six weeks!

FRED. Aye, I expect it would be wearing a bit thin by then. Ee,
but you surprise me, love, for I'd have said Arthur would be off the
mark like a shot.

VIOLET. Well, yes . . . when we were courting there were times
I could hardly hold him in check. And now it's come to this.

FRED. Well, it's not as rare as you seem to think. I reckon it
happens to every man some time or other . . . but to know it's been

going on with you and Arthur for six weeks has given me quite a shock.

VIOLET. Not half the shock it's given Arthur. He can't get over it. He's made me feel worse. It all seemed to go wrong from our wedding night when Joe Thompson played that dirty trick with the bed.

FRED. Silly twit.

VIOLET. Ee, I'd love to paste his lug for him. But Arthur should be over that setback by this. What can be the cause of it all, Uncle Fred?

FRED. It could be anything, love. It could be worry—worry about his job, about not being able to get a home together, about . . .

VIOLET (cuts in) Uncle Fred, you don't think Arthur might be one of those men who can't find happiness with a woman?

FRED. Can't find happiness with a woman!—what man can!—or without one, either. But if you mean what I think you mean, the answer is no. What put that daft idea into your head?

VIOLET. You think of everything when you're lying awake at night.

FRED. Well, take my word for it that Arthur is not one of them. And if he were it wouldn't be as though he could help it. Anyway, what are we going on about Arthur for all the time—it might not be his fault.

VIOLET. Whose else? It must be his fault. By all accounts it's a straightforward business—and after all, I'm only the woman.

(*A testy note of challenge is getting into it as* FRED *defends Arthur*)

FRED. Only! Speaking as a bachelor I'd say the woman was most important. Love isn't a one-sided business—she's got to know how to play her part.

VIOLET. But it's supposed to come natural, isn't it . . . after all, it is an instinct.

FRED. Yes . . . eating's an instinct too, love—only some cooks are better than others.

VIOLET. Yes, but you need something to cook with, don't you. I can't see any way out of it . . . I mean Arthur seems to be getting tensed up all the time.

FRED. Can you blame him—in these surroundings.

VIOLET. Well, they're not so bad. And I mean it is his own home.

FRED. Nay, it's not his home, it's his dad's. And what might suit you as a single chap can put you off once you're married.

VIOLET. Other couples manage.

FRED. All couples are not alike. A man can't just go off like an alarm clock. It depends on him being at ease. If he's content in his mind, a man can make love on dry bread and cold water. But if he's not, champagne and oysters won't help. And the place is so small, he's got no privacy. There's you two in one bedroom, his mum and dad in the next—he must feel his life's not his own.

VIOLET. Yes, it is cramped . . . and Arthur's got this thing about his father.

FRED. Aye, I noticed that at the wedding . . . they seemed to be at sixes and sevens.

VIOLET. It's not that they don't like each other—it's just that they can't strike it off.

FRED. Ezra seems to get on better with Geoffrey.

VIOLET (*brightens*) Oh, everybody gets on with Geoffrey. He's always so cheerful and he doesn't seem to take things to heart like Arthur.

FRED. Reckon you get on well with him, too?

VIOLET. Oh, like a house on fire. He's so helpful—and always so nice. I don't know what I'd do without Geoff round the place.

(FRED *has been watching Violet closely*)

FRED (*looks at his watch*) I suppose I'd best be making off. I don't seem to have been of much help. Violet, I was just thinking . . . are you sure you've married the right brother?

VIOLET (*astonished*) Married the right brother . . . ! But of course I have! What gave *you* that daft idea? I wouldn't swop Arthur for a dozen Geoffreys. Getting on with somebody is one thing . . . loving them is quite another. I love Arthur . . . and I don't care what happens or what doesn't, I shall love him till my dying day.

(FRED *has registered some surprise and ended up with more understanding after this outburst*)

FRED. Love . . . I reckon that's your answer. With love behind you, it'll all come right—(*he kisses Violet good-bye*)—perhaps when you least expect it. (*He moves towards the door*) Good-bye, chick, and good luck.

VIOLET. God bless, Uncle Fred.

FRED. Don't lose heart—keep your faith . . . love has its own way of fixing things . . . you'll see. . . .

(FRED *exits*)

VIOLET. Well, all I can say is—it's taking it a damn long time . . . !

CURTAIN

ACT II

SCENE 3

SCENE—*The Fitton home. The same evening.*

ARTHUR *is seated at the table, reading, with his book propped up against his mug of tea.* EDDIE *enters from the back kitchen, with teapot.*

EDDIE. More tea, Arthur?

(ARTHUR *doesn't answer*)

I said, more tea!

ARTHUR (*without looking up*) I don't mind, if there's any left.

(EDDIE *pours tea*)

EDDIE. I've just filled the pot. Has your dad gone to the Wanderers then?

ARTHUR (*without looking up*) I suppose so.

EDDIE (*tries again*) And your mum to the market?

ARTHUR (*reads on*) ... Aye ...

EDDIE (*still trying*) And Violet's not back yet. ...

ARTHUR (*gives ironical look round*) ... No ... I don't think so. ...
(*Continues to read*)

EDDIE (*tries new tack*) By the way, Arthur—how's married life going?

ARTHUR (*looks up*) What?

EDDIE. I say, married life—how's it going?

ARTHUR (*pause*) Not so bad—why?

EDDIE. Nothing—I were just asking.

ARTHUR. But why were you asking about married life? Any particular reason?

EDDIE (*explodes*) No particular reason! I were just bloody asking —that's all! But the way it's got with you lately, nobody can say a word to you without you picking 'um up! I don't know what the hell's got into you!

ARTHUR (*grins*) Sorry, Eddy. I don't know why I came over so humpty.

EDDIE (*joking*) Well, keep a better hold on yourself or else ...

(EDDIE *shakes his fist at Athur, mock threatening*)

ARTHUR (*closes the book*) Aye, I'd better. I suppose it's time we were getting back to work.

EDDIE (*looks at his watch*) We're all right yet awhile.

(*There is a loud knocking at the door*)

JOE (*calls off*) Aye! Aye! Anybody at home!

EDDIE. It's Joe Thompson—bloody cheek.

(JOE THOMPSON *enters. He is dressed up and self-important*)

JOE. I thought I'd find you here! Come on—let's be having you. Back to work.

ARTHUR. We were just coming.

JOE. Well, come on then ... don't hang it out here. Back in the box. The customers are in and waiting.

EDDIE. We were just finishing our teatime.

JOE. You don't want all flamin' day for your tea. What do you think I'm paying you for? Come on, Fitton.

ARTHUR. I'm coming—but don't you come barging in here like that.

EDDIE. By rights, Mr Thompson, our tea half-hour isn't up yet.

JOE. Don't you be so bloody cheeky. Come on.

ARTHUR. Are you sure, Eddie?

EDDIE. I'm certain. Positive. We broke at five. Now it's five an' twenty past. We've another five minutes by rights.

(ARTHUR *sits down, opens his book, and starts reading.* EDDIE *laughs at the sight.* JOE *turns on Eddie*)

JOE. You get back. (*To Arthur*) Fitton, what the hell's come over you? What do you think you're at?

ARTHUR. I'm just finishing my tea hour.

EDDIE. Aye, we've still—— (*Looks at his watch*)

JOE (*roars at Eddie*) You get back! Go on! Or else . . .

(EDDIE *makes to go*)

ARTHUR. I wouldn't go if I were you, Eddie—I'd insist on my rights.

JOE (*to Arthur*) Rights—you're a nice bloody one to talk about folks' rights . . .

(ARTHUR *detects some underlying meaning*)

ARTHUR. What do you mean—eh?

JOE. Aw, forget it, forget it. Now let's be having you—get cracking—you don't want me to do your job for you, d'you?

ARTHUR. Why—d'you think you could!

JOE. Do your job! (*He cackles*) I'd do it on my bloody head! (*To Eddie*) You get back when I tell you!

EDDIE (*looks at his watch*) We've still another four minutes.

JOE. Yes, on my bloody head.

ARTHUR. That's what you say!

JOE. And come to think of it, Fitton, I reckon I could do another little job for you as well. (*To Eddie*) Will you get back when you're told!

(ARTHUR *goes quietly over to Joe*)

EDDIE. What's he getting at, Arthur?

ARTHUR. Yes . . . what do you mean—what job?

JOE. Never mind what job—(*he cackles*)—just send for me next time.

(EDDIE *spots Arthur's tenseness and goes quiet*)

ARTHUR. Send for you—send for you for what?

JOE. To do a job for that little wife of yours, Violet—that's for what—one it seems you haven't got around to doing yet. (*To Eddie*) Get back in there. (*To Arthur*) You talking about your rights—what about her bloody rights, eh? The wife's rights—her conjugal rights! (*He cackles*) Her right to have a bit of the old . . .

(ARTHUR *has grabbed Joe near the throat and shakes him. with such force that he knocks him breathless*)

ARTHUR. You filthy swine! I'll . . .
JOE. You're choking me! Let go—you're choking me!
ARTHUR. I'll choke you, you bastard . . .

(*He pushes Joe back. A chair falls over which Eddie picks up*)

EDDIE (*whispered support*) Go on, Arthur . . . belt him!

(*During this there is a loud knocking at the door which is ignored, and* MOLLY *enters*)

ARTHUR. Take it back. . . .
MOLLY (*calls*) Joe, are you . . . ! (*Spots the fight going on and stops dead*) Bloody hell—what's up!
JOE (*choking*) Let go!

(ARTHUR *draws his right fist back, still holding Joe and is about to hit him*)

ARTHUR. Take it back—what you said—or I'll. . . .

(JOE *continues to make choking sounds*)

MOLLY. Stop it! Stop it! Let go of him.

(MOLLY *grabs hold of Arthur*)

Can you hear me? Let go! You'll choke him. Have you gone mad!
EDDIE. Go on! Give it to him, Arthur!
ARTHUR (*ignoring Molly*) Take it back—take back what you said
—apologize or I'll . . .
JOE (*finally*) Sorry. (*Choking*) I apologize, blast you!

(ARTHUR *lets go with a jerk.* JOE *staggers, nursing his throat*)

MOLLY. What's been going on here? (*To Arthur*) Hy, you nearly choked him. (*To Eddie*) What's it all about—what happened?
EDDIE. That'll stop him bringing your wife up, Arthur.
JOE (*to Eddie*) You get back to your work.
MOLLY (*to Eddie*) What happened—I'm asking you what happened?
EDDIE. He said something about Arthur and Violet.
ARTHUR. And I'm just warning you—if ever you dare mention my wife's name again I'll sort you out proper. . . .

(JOE *backs away from Arthur*)

JOE. You get back to your work when I tell you!
MOLLIE (*to Eddie*) What did he say!
EDDIE. Something about doing a job for him. Send for me next time, he said. It upset Arthur.
MOLLY. The ignorant sod! Ee, I'm right sorry, Arthur, that he'd say anything about you and that lovely little girl you married.

JOE. Fitton, you're sacked—that's your lot.

ARTHUR. Oh, stuff your bloody job.

(ARTHUR *exits*)

JOE (*roars at Eddie*) You get back to your work.

EDDIE (*calmly looking at his watch*) I've another minute and a half yet.

MOLLY (*upset*) You promised you would never breathe a word, didn't you—and the first one you tell is the poor lad himself.

JOE. He drew it out of me.

MOLLY. Drew it out of you—I wish I'd let him choke you—to say a thing like that. As if things weren't difficult enough for them. (*She pauses*) You do a job for Arthur—you—you flamin' old two in one, why you couldn't do a job for our cat—you're all talk—all bloody talk. I've a good mind to . . . (*She sets about Joe with her handbag*) You do a job—you wouldn't know where to start—you—why, the flaming laundryman has been doing a job for you for years! An' doing it better than you'd know how!

JOE *yells out as* MOLLY *lamblasts him, and* EDDIE *cheers and tidies up behind them and follows them off, as lights* BLACK-OUT *and—*

the CURTAIN *falls*

Continue with Scene 4 as printed except on pages 55–56 but **cut**
VIOLET. Arthur! What are you saying?
to
ARTHUR. What? To talk me over with the family quack?

also cut "tell anybody" from the end of VIOLET (*very upset for Arthur*), Oh, Arthur, I'm so sorry, etc.

and alter "told him" to "told 'em" in ARTHUR. Liar! Bloody liar! etc.

FURNITURE AND PROPERTY LIST

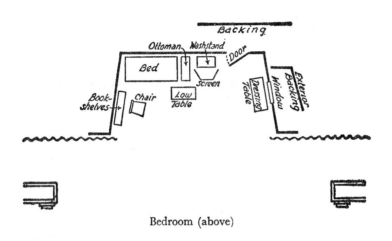

Bedroom (above)

Living room (below)

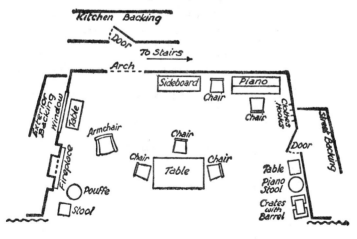

ACT I

SCENE 1

On stage: *In the living room:*

Stool (down R) *On it:* book for Arthur

Pouffe (down R)

Firegrate

Fender

Hearth rug

Poker

Over mantelpiece: mirror

On mantelpiece: ornaments, pipe-cleaners in vase, pouch with tobacco, ashtray, matches

Shelf. *On it:* plates, jugs, vase, gas-meter

Leather armchair. *On it:* antimacassar

Table. *On it:* TV set

Sideboard. *On it:* lace cover, ornaments, parcel of sheets tied with blue ribbon, table-lamp, iron box, bottle of port, 2 glasses, plate with piece of wedding cake, list of names, wedding-cake boxes, ashtray.

      In drawers: clean folded tea towel, hand towel, handkerchief

      In cupboard: 6 cups, 6 saucers, white quart jug, 4 glasses

Over sideboard: 4 pictures

Chair (R of piano) *On it:* Leslie's jacket with carnation

Chair (at piano)

Piano. *On it:* plate with tomato sandwich, picture of dogs, quart bottle of beer, 3 glasses, candelabra, ashtray, 3 port glasses, brass jug with flowers, concertina

On floor L of piano: shopping basket

Table (c) *On it:* cloth, Molly's handbag, glass of beer for Fred

3 upright chairs

Clothes pegs (L) *On them:* coats, etc., for Leslie, Liz, Joe, Molly, Fred and Eddie

Coffee-table (L) *On it:* record player, pint glass of beer, ashtray

      On shelf: transistor radio, magazine, newspapers

Piano stool (down L)

Beer keg on 2 crates, gallon, white jug, glass

Carpet

Window curtains

Light pendant

Light switch up R

In the bedroom:

Bookshelves (R) *On them:* bedside light, bunch of roses in tissue paper

      In them: books and magazines

Upright chair
Bedside rug
Bed (set to collapse) *On it:* mattress, sheets, pillows, blanket, bedspread, Violet's nightdress, Arthur's pyjamas, wedding veil
Under bed: Arthur's slippers
Box ottoman
On wall R: 4 Medici Gallery postcards
On back wall over bed: framed picture of a galleon
Shelf. *On it:* tumbler, shaving brush, shaving stick, etc.
Washstand. *On it:* enamel bowl with water carafe, towel
  Under it: white enamel jug of water
Screen with postcards and pictures
Curtain for door
On door: Arthur's dressing-gown
Rug (LC)
Window curtains
Dressing-table with mirror. *On it:* lace cover, toilet articles, brush and comb, Kleenex, ashtray, packet of cigarettes, matches
  In drawer: Arthur's white shirt
Coffee-table. *On it:* tape recorder, 4 tape boxes
Light switch R of door

Off stage: Wedding cake with piece cut out (LESLIE)
  Tray. *On it:* pot of tea, tea cosy, jug of milk, bowl of sugar, 11 cups, 11 saucers, 11 teaspoons (LUCY)
  Large plate, knife (VIOLET)
  Jug of hot water (MOLLY)
  Spanner (JOE)

Personal: JOE: gaudy handkerchief, cigars, matches
  GEOFFREY: half-crown
  MOLLY: handbag. *In it:* compact
  LIZ: handbag. *In it:* handkerchief
  LESLIE: pipe, tobacco, matches, half-crown
  ARTHUR: carnation buttonhole

SCENE 2

Strike: *From bedroom:*
  Roses
  Wedding dress, etc.

SCENE 3

Strike: *From living-room:*
  Dirty glasses
  Dirty crockery
  Crates and barrel
  Wedding cake, etc.
Tidy room generally

Set: *On table* c: check cloth, large plate, dirtied, with knife and fork, 2
        mugs, pot of marmalade with spoon, cruet, plate of bread and
        butter, plate with bacon sandwich, sheet of greaseproof paper,
        2 knives, 2 forks, jug of milk, sugar basin, ashtray
       On sideboard: glass bowl with fruit, vase of flowers, cup and saucer,
        wedding photograph, crash helmet, gloves, tray
       On pegs L: Ezra's cap, overalls and raincoat, Lucy's coat
       On armchair: scarf, leather jacket
       In hearth: pot of tea and tea cosy
       On back of chair L: Ezra's jacket

Off stage: Towel (EZRA)
            Towel, sponge bag. *In it:* hairbrush, comb, scent spray (VIOLET)
            Tray. *On it:* sugar basin, plate with 2 apples (VIOLET)
            2 cups of coffee, toast (VIOLET)
            Insurance book (LIZ)
            Death certificate (LIZ)
            Attache case (LESLIE)

Personal: LIZ: handbag. *In it:* cigarettes, matches

ACT II

SCENE 1

Strike: Check cloth and remaining breakfast things from table
          Towels
          Sponge bag
          Attache case
          Insurance book
          Death certificate
          TV set

Set: *On table:* cornet and polishing cloth
       On armchair: sewing for Lucy

Off stage: White quart jug of beer (EZRA)
            4 small bottles stout (EZRA)

Personal: EZRA: pipe, tobacco, matches, spectacles, spectacle case
            LESLIE: pipe, tobacco, matches
            LIZ: handkerchief

SCENE 2

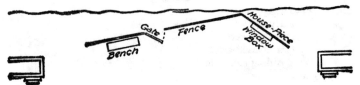

On stage: Bench
Window-box. *In it:* 3 potted geraniums
Rabbit hutch with rabbit

Off stage: Bowl with lettuce leaves and clover (**FRED**)
Photograph album (VIOLET)

SCENE 3

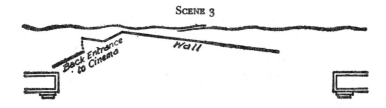

Off stage: Ball (EDDIE)

Personal: JOE: cigarettes, matches
EDDIE: watch
MOLLY: handbag

SCENE 4

Setting as Act II, Scene 1
Set: *On table:* check cloth, 2 cups, 2 saucers, 2 side plates, 2 mugs, jug of
milk, plate with bread and butter, jar of jam, 3 large knives,
3 large forks, dessert spoon, bowl of sugar, bottle of sauce, plate
with tomatoes, copy of the *Bolton Evening News*, plate of bubble and
squeak, plate of cake
In bedroom: *On ottoman:* canvas grip
On bed: shirt, pyjamas

Off stage: Pot of tea (LUCY)
Raincoat (ARTHUR)
Parcel. *In it:* cage with 2 love-birds (GEOFFREY)
Raincoat, scarf (GEOFFREY)
Plate of sausage and mash (LUCY)
Suitcase (ARTHUR)
Coat and handbag (VIOLET)

Personal: EZRA: banknotes, spectacles, pipe
GEOFFREY: 2 tickets

Any character costumes or wigs needed in the performance of
this play can be hired from CHARLES H. Fox Ltd, 25 Shelton
Street, London WC2H 9HX

LIGHTING PLOT

Property fittings required: shaded pendant, table-lamp, firegrate, bedside
  light
  Interior. A living-room and a bedroom.
  THE APPARENT SOURCES are, in daytime, in the living-room, a window
    R and in the bedroom, a window L. At night: in the living-room, a
    shaded pendant C and a table-lamp up L, and in the bedroom, a
    bedside light R
  THE MAIN ACTING AREA covers the whole stage

ACT I, SCENE 1. Night

To open: The bedroom in darkness
  In the living-room: fittings on
  fire on

Cue 1	GEOFFREY switches off lights	(Page 11)
	Snap out fittings	
	Snap out covering lights	
Cue 2	JOE switches on bedroom lights	(Page 11)
	Snap in bedroom fitting	
	Snap in covering lights	
Cue 3	EDDIE switches out bedroom light	(Page 12)
	Snap out bedroom fitting	
	Snap out covering lights	
Cue 4	GEOFFREY switches on living-room lights	(Page 12)
	Snap in fittings	
	Snap in covering lights	
Cue 5	EZRA switches out living-room lights	(Page 20)
	Snap out fittings	
	Snap out covering lights	
Cue 6	ARTHUR switches on bedroom light	(Page 20)
	Snap in bedroom fitting	
	Snap in covering lights	
Cue 7	ARTHUR: ". . . rest of them."	(Page 23)
	BLACK-OUT	

ACT I, SCENE 2. Night

To open: The living-room in darkness
  The bedroom dimly lit
  Bedroom fitting on

Cue 8	VIOLET: "I love you."	(Page 26)
	Snap in light behind glass panel in bedroom door	

Cue 9	VIOLET switches off lamp *Snap out bedroom fitting* *Snap out covering lights*	(Page 26)
Cue 10	EZRA: "... round your side." BLACK-OUT	(Page 26)

ACT I, SCENE 3. Morning

To open: Effect of daylight in living-room
Bedroom in darkness
Fittings off
Fire on

No cues

ACT II, SCENE 1. Evening

To open: The bedroom in darkness
In the living-room: fittings on
fire on

Cue 11	LUCY: "... find out, love." BLACK-OUT	(Page 47)

ACT II, SCENE 2. Exterior

To open: Effect of dull daylight

Cue 12	FRED: "Eh, Flossie?" BLACK-OUT	(Page 50)

ACT II, SCENE 3. Exterior

To open: Effect of sunshine

Cue 13	EDDIE exits BLACK-OUT	(Page 53)

ACT II, SCENE 4

To open: The bedroom in darkness
In the living-room: fittings on
fire on

Cue 14	LUCY: "... upset our Arthur." *Fade lights on living-room* *Bring up lights on bedroom*	(Page 55)
Cue 15	ARTHUR: "I'll—I'll ..." *Fade lights on bedroom* *Bring up lights on living-room*	(Page 56)

EFFECTS PLOT

ACT I

SCENE 1

SCENE 3

Cue 15	At rise of CURTAIN	(Page 27)
	Sound of factory buzzers and hooters and other industrial noises	
Cue 16	GEOFFREY exits	(Page 27)
	Sound of a motor cycle starting up and driving away	
Cue 17	EZRA: ". . . I'm just going."	(Page 28)
	Sound of factory buzzer	
Cue 18	ARTHUR switches on transistor	(Page 30)
	Music of Mozart's "Eine Kleine Nacht Musik"	
Cue 19	ARTHUR switches off transistor	(Page 30)
	Stop music	
Cue 20	VIOLET: ". . . he said anything?"	(Page 31)
	Mozart music recommences upstairs	
Cue 21	VIOLET brushes her hair	(Page 31)
	Sound of kettle whistling	
Cue 22	VIOLET: ". . . cup of coffee."	(Page 32)
	Music ceases	

ACT II

SCENE 1

No cues

SCENE 2

Cue 23	FRED: ". . . you need."	(Page 50)
	Sound of motor cycle horn	
Cue 24	VIOLET exits	(Page 50)
	Start of motor cycle starting up and driving away	

SCENE 3

No cues

SCENE 4

Cue 25	GEOFFREY removes cover of birdcage	(Page 58)
	Sound of bird song	
Cue 26	VIOLET: "Listen to 'em, Arthur."	(Page 65)
	Sound of bird song	
Cue 27	EZRA: ". . . you bloody cry."	(Page 66)
	Sound *of bird song*	

MADE AND PRINTED IN GREAT BRITAIN BY
LATIMER TREND & COMPANY LTD PLYMOUTH

MADE IN ENGLAND